EXPLORATIONS

STUDIES IN CULTURE AND COMMUNICATION

VOLUME 1

Edited by Edmund Carpenter and Marshall McLuhan

WIPF & STOCK · Eugene, Oregon

Wipf and Stock Publishers
199 W 8th Ave, Suite 3
Eugene, OR 97401

Explorations 1
Studies in Culture and Communication
By Carpenter, E S and Easterbrook, W T

ISBN 13: 978-1-62032-427-1
Publication date 9/22/2016
Previously published by University of Toronto, 1953

This is an anniversary new edition of the eight co-edited issues of Explorations, with annotations by Michael Darroch and Janine Marchessault, in conjunction with students and researchers at the University of Windsor and York University, Canada. Research for the annotated editions was made possible by a grant from the Social Sciences and Humanities Research Council of Canada. Additional research was provided by Lorraine Spiess in conjunction with the Estate of Edmund Carpenter. Permissions research was provided by Jonathan McKenzie. This republication project was a joint initiative undertaken by the estates of Marshall McLuhan and Edmund Carpenter.

Funding for Issues 1–6 (1953–1956) was originally provided by a grant from the Ford Foundation's Behavioral Sciences Program. Issues 7–8 (1957) were sponsored by the Telegram of Toronto.

Typography for Issue 1 was designed and printed by Rous & Mann Press Limited, Toronto. The cover of Issue 7 and the cover and typography of Issue 8 were designed by Harley Parker and printed courtesy of the University of Toronto Press. Please see individual issues for further notes on contributors and acknowledgements.

EXPLORATIONS . . .

is designed, not as a permanent reference journal that embalms truth for posterity, but as a publication that explores and searches and questions.

We envisage a series that will cut across the humanities and social sciences by treating them as a continuum. We believe anthropology and communication are approaches, not bodies of data, and that within each the four winds of the humanities, the physical, the biological and the social sciences intermingle to form a science of man.

Volumes 1 through 6:

Editor:
E. S. Carpenter
Associate Editors:
W. T. Easterbrook
H. M. McLuhan
J. Tyrwhitt
D. C. Williams

Address all correspondence to EXPLORATIONS
University of Toronto
Toronto, Canada

Volumes 7 & 8:

Editors:
Edmund Carpenter
Marshall McLuhan

Sponsor Telegram of Toronto
Publisher University of Toronto

December 1953

Explorations, 1953–57

Introduction to the Eight-Volume Series of the 2016 Edition

Michael Darroch (University of Windsor) and
Janine Marchessault (York University)

"TV Wollops the MS! The monopoly of knowledge enjoyed by print for centuries was destroyed by the mass media. After a beating by radio and movies, MS was knocked cold by TV. Observers predict that before a staggering comeback, book culture must train in a fresh air camp."[1]

So claimed an inconspicuous headline in the inside rear cover of the second issue of the journal *Explorations*, published in April 1954. The front and rear covers depicted a spoof newspaper whose main headline pronounced, "Feenicht's Playhouse: New Media Changing Temporal-Spatial Orientation to Self." Now in full swing, *Explorations*—an experimental interdisciplinary publication led by faculty and graduate students at the University of Toronto—would become the forum in which Marshall McLuhan and Edmund Carpenter formulated their most striking insights about new media in the electric age.

Explorations was not the first humanistic journal on a quest to discover common vocabularies between arts and sciences. It was, however, the first such endeavour to emerge from an interdisciplinary research team striving to understand the implications of postwar new media of communication: photography, film, radio, television, even early computing. The team included McLuhan—a little-known English professor who had arrived at the

1. Inside back cover, April 1954, *Explorations* 2. Carpenter and McLuhan drew inspiration from A. Irving Hallowell's considerations of "spatio-temporal orientation" in his extensive essay titled "The Self and its Behavioral Environment." See Carpenter to Hallowell, 20 January 1954. Alfred Hallowell Papers, Series 1. American Philosophical Society, Philadelphia.

University of Toronto in 1946 eager to build a network of scholars invested in studying the materiality of media across historical and contemporary popular cultures—and Carpenter, an ambitious anthropologist studying concepts of space and time among indigenous peoples, especially the Aivilik Inuit, and moonlighting as a radio and TV broadcaster at the Canadian Broadcasting Corporation.

Carpenter recalled meeting McLuhan at his Toronto home in 1948 as a momentous encounter. He had been teaching in the University of Toronto's anthropology department while writing his dissertation on the prehistory of Northeast indigenous cultures at the University of Pennsylvania. A lifelong friendship based on lively intellectual exchange developed between the two men. Besides being junior faculty members, they had much in common: an interest in new media, and the impact of these media on the human sensorium and forms of education and knowledge. Perhaps most centrally, they shared a profound disdain for the confining strictures of disciplinary specialisms which universities were increasingly fostering. Together they hatched a plan for a landmark think tank that would develop interdisciplinary methodologies and new vocabularies needed to make sense of the changing mediated environments of postwar North America. The group further included Jaqueline Tyrwhitt, a British town planner with ties to the Bauhaus and the British wing of CIAM or the *Congrès internationaux d'architecture moderne*, which had been launched in 1928 by Le Corbusier and Sigfried Giedion, both of whom had been major inspirations to McLuhan since the early 1940s.[2] Thomas Easterbrook, a political economist and longtime friend of McLuhan, was deeply conversant with his mentor Harold A. Innis's studies of cultural economies, ancient civilizations, and their related patterns of communication and media biases across space and time. D. Carlton Williams, a psychologist rising in the university's administration who was acquainted with mass communications research and contemporaneous studies of human sense perception, brought a scientific perspective to research. The plan for a think tank—an "experiment in communication"[3]—would lead to the Culture and Communications graduate seminar (1953–55), innovative media experiments, talks and conferences, and the crowning achievement, the journal *Explorations: Studies in Culture and Communication*. The eight

2. See Darroch, 2008; Darroch & Marchessault, 2009; Geiser, 2010; Darroch, 2014; Darroch, 2016a; Darroch, 2016b.

3. Matie Molinaro, Corinne McLuhan, and William Toye (Eds.), *Letters of Marshall McLuhan*, Toronto: Oxford University Press, 1987: 223.

coedited issues of *Explorations* are republished here for the first time since their original printing in the 1950s.

The Explorations research group aimed to develop a "field approach" to the study of new media and communication. While inspired by a postwar, modernist discourse of universality, no single mode of research was dominant. By their own account, the team sought "an area of mutually supporting insights in a critique of the methods of study in Economics, Psychology, English, Anthropology, and Town Planning."[4] The journal's masthead (for the first six issues) would declare that *Explorations* "is designed, not as a permanent reference journal that embalms truth for posterity, but as a publication that explores and searches and questions. We envisage a series that will cut across the humanities and social sciences by treating them as a continuum. We believe anthropology and communication are approaches, not bodies of data, and that within each the four winds of the humanities, the physical, the biological and the social sciences intermingle to form a science of man."[5]

This series description was in part lifted from the short-lived interdisciplinary journal *trans/formation: arts, communication, environment*, a publication rooted in modernist discourse and edited by New York abstract artist Harry Holtzman, the champion of Piet Mondrian's legacy in the United States. *trans/formation*, which folded after only three issues had been published between 1950 and 1952 (all three of which were held in the Toronto seminar's "library"), counted Tyrwhitt and Giedion among its contributing editors[6] and sought to bridge disciplinary boundaries, not by attempting to synthesize ideas into a single perspective but rather by arranging myriad concepts into new dynamic patterns and configurations.[7] *trans/formation*'s masthead "affirmed that art, science, and technology are interacting components of the total human enterprise . . . but today they are too often

4. Herbert Marshall McLuhan Fonds, held in Library and Archives Canada (LAC) in Ottawa. Further references to the McLuhan Fonds will be identified as LAC followed by the call number MG 31, D 156, the volume number, and the folder number (here: LAC MG 31, D 156, 145, 35).

5. Front matter, December 1953–June 1956, *Explorations* 1–6.

6. The list also included Le Corbusier, Marcel Duchamp, Buckminster Fuller, György Kepes, and S. I. Hayakawa, among many others.

7. See Anna Vallye, 2009, "The Strategic Universality of *trans/formation*, 1950–1952," *Grey Room* 35:28–57.

treated as if they were cultural isolates and mutually antagonistic. Lack of time, misinformation, specialised terminology make it hard to keep pace with advances in all fields."[8] Indeed, *trans/formation*'s stated intention "to cut across the arts and sciences by treating them as a continuum" was a clear inspiration for *Explorations*. McLuhan himself suggested to Tyrwhitt, "Perhaps we might use some of the *Transformation* material if there is to be no 4th issue there?"[9] Tyrwhitt would later contribute a paper she had drafted for *trans/formation*, "Ideal Cities and the City Ideal," to *Explorations* 2, tracing histories of utopian thought in urban studies.[10]

Explorations published writings by group members along with contributions on topics ranging from ethnolinguistics to economic theory, from art and design to developmental psychology, from psychoanalysis to nursery rhymes and bawdy ballads, from urban theory to electronic media. The journal treated culture, and cultural studies, as a landscape of experiences and knowledge. An experimental space in its own right, *Explorations* counted among its more than eighty contributors both established and emerging scholars, scientists, and artists.

Perhaps the most representative issue of *Explorations* was number 4, published in February 1955, where poems by e. e. cummings and Jorge Luis Borges mingled with essays by McLuhan on "Space, Time, and Poetry," Carpenter on "Eskimo Poetry: Word Magic," Tyrwhitt on "The Moving Eye" (regarding cinematic experiences of urban life and comparative perceptions of ancient cities in India), and Williams on "auditory space"—a notion that "electrified" the group, as Carpenter later recounted.[11] Essays by literary scholar Northrop Frye on "The Language of Poetry" and anthropologist Dorothy Lee on "Freedom, Spontaneity and Limit in American Linguistic Usage" were juxtaposed with case studies by graduate students at the time, such as English and communications scholar Walter J. Ong on "Space in Renaissance Symbolism" and anthropologist Joan Rayfield on "Some Im-

8. Front matter, 1950, *trans/formation: arts, communication, environment* 1.

9. Marshall McLuhan to Jaqueline Tyrwhitt, 8 December 1953. Papers of Jaqueline Tyrwhitt (1885–1980). Royal Institute of British Architects, TYJ/18. RIBA British Architectural Library Drawings and Archives Collection, London.

10. Ellen Shoshkes, 2014, *Jaqueline Tyrwhitt: A Transnational Life in Urban Planning and Design,* Farnham, UK: Ashgate: 147.

11. Edmund Carpenter, 2001, "That Not-So-Silent Sea," in Donald F. Theall (Ed.), The Virtual Marshall McLuhan (pp. 241), Montreal: McGill-Queen's University Press.

plications of English Grammar." A "Media Log," largely replicated from McLuhan's 1954 version of *Counterblast*, was published in addition to an "Idea File" containing insights on oral, written, and technological cultural forms culled from writings by Robert Graves, Edmund Leach, Walter Gropius, and E. T. Hall, among many others. *Explorations* 4 boldly announced the fledgling field of media studies as deeply rooted in anthropological and literary-poetic traditions, but equally informed by studies of mechanisation, technology, and culture. As Carpenter and McLuhan surmised, it was an interdisciplinary and experimental framework that was needed for studying contemporary culture: a problem "requiring a harmony of the arts and behavioral sciences" and an "orchestration of diverse techniques."[12]

Ford Foundation

Through a grant application in 1953 to the Ford Foundation's newly established interdisciplinary research and study program in behavioral sciences (most likely cowritten by McLuhan and Carpenter and assisted by the then doctoral student Donald Theall, but submitted under the names of all five team members), the group obtained $44,250 for a two-year research project devoted to studying the "changing patterns of language and behavior and the new media of communication."[13] With the Culture and Communication Seminar, the group proposed to meet the specific criteria of the new Ford program by establishing a kind of think tank for faculty and graduate students to tackle the specific circumstances fostered by the new media of the 1950s. As the program pamphlet explained, it was expected that the "direction of the project would be assumed jointly by a behavioral scientist and by a scholar from a related discipline" to conduct "research on a problem requiring their collaboration." They "would organize a joint seminar, either

12. Edmund S. Carpenter, Jaqueline Tyrwhitt, H. M. McLuhan, W. T. Easterbrook, and D. C. Williams, 1953, "University of Toronto: Changing Patterns of Language and Behavior and the New Media of Communication," Ford Foundation Archives, New York: Rockefeller Archive Center. Grant File PA 53–70, Section 1, 1–11, here page 3.

13. *Ford Foundation*, 1953, *Ford Foundation Annual Report 1953*, New York: Ford Foundation: 67. The Ford Foundation's Behavioral Sciences Program had the stated goal of "improving the content of the behavioral sciences" by specifically supporting "interdisciplinary research and study." Launched in 1952, the program aimed to help the "intellectual development of the behavioral sciences" by "improving their relationship with such disciplines as history, social and political philosophy, humanistic studies and certain phases of economics" (67).

formal or informal, dealing not only with the particular problem under study but also with the general problems of cross-disciplinary work involved. Faculty members and graduate students from the different fields of specialization would participate in both the research project and the seminar."[14] In many ways, the program echoed scholars such as Sigfried Giedion, who had long advocated for "Chairs" or "Faculties of Interrelations" at universities in Europe and North America.[15] Within North America, the Toronto group's proposal can be counted among the very first attempts to combine explicitly the study of culture *and* communication. The timing of this grant is significant given the scope of contemporaneous studies of media underway in the United States and Europe: functionalist and critical cultural studies of mass communications, theories of cybernetics, studies of social interaction, as well as psychological studies of the effects of media on human perception. Carpenter, initially the driving force behind *Explorations*, acted as editor of the first six issues—the issues funded through the Ford grant—before becoming coeditor with McLuhan for issues 7 and 8, which were sponsored by the *Toronto Telegram*. A ninth and final issue, entitled *Eskimo* (1959), combined Carpenter's writings on indigenous art and culture of the Aivilik juxtaposed with images from filmmaker Robert Flaherty and drawings by Frederick Varley. After Beacon Press published a selection of *Explorations* contributions in 1960, coedited by Carpenter and McLuhan as *Explorations in Communication*, McLuhan later resuscitated the spirit of *Explorations* as a "magazine within a magazine," a publication inside the University of Toronto's alumni magazine, the *Varsity Graduate* (1964–72).

The group's proposal to Ford's Behavioral Sciences Program is revealing of the central assumptions that would underpin the graduate seminar and *Explorations*. The proposal's point of departure is not yet an assumption about the power of media forms to shape content, but rather the understanding that methods for studying new media required recognition of new patterns emerging across technological, cultural, and urban life. Underpinning the proposal is a conversation that McLuhan in particular had started with advocates of cybernetic theories. Carpenter was also of course conversant with the writings of anthropologists who were deeply involved with developing

14. "Announcement of Interdisciplinary Research and Study Program." Ford Foundation, Behavioral Sciences Division. LAC MG 31 156 204 26.

15. See Sigfried Giedion, 1987, "A Faculty of Interrelations," in D. Huber (Ed.), *Wege in die Öffentlichkeit* (pp. 160–63), Zurich: Institut für Geschichte und Theorie der Architektur.

cybernetic models and metaphors within the social sciences, among others Gregory Bateson and Margaret Mead. Cybernetic theories also came to the group through Donald Theall, who would complete his PhD dissertation in 1954 on "Communication Theories in Modern Poetry: Yeats, Pound, Joyce and Eliot" under the supervision of both McLuhan and Carpenter. In the December 1949 issue of the *Yale Scientific Magazine*, Theall had reviewed Norbert Wiener's *Cybernetics: Or Control and Communication in the Animal and the Machine* (1948), and with Carpenter he would introduce McLuhan to Gregory Bateson and Jurgen Ruesch's *Communication: The Social Matrix of Psychiatry* (1951). Bateson and Ruesch's book drew substantially on Wiener's cybernetics and Gestalt psychology's concept of pattern formation, while offering a distinctly interdisciplinary range of approaches to understanding the individual self within a variety of social constellations. McLuhan and Carpenter turned to these texts as well as the writings of political theorist Karl W. Deutsch, a key proponent of social science interpretations of cybernetic theories emanating from the writings of Wiener and the famous "Macy Conferences" at MIT (1946–53) in his essays on communication and information theory, social organizations, and the need for a new unity of knowledge in higher education.[16] Citing Deutsch (although without reference), their final Ford proposal begins with the statement that "communications engineering does not transfer events, commodities, or services but a patterned relationship between these."[17] The authors then quickly suggest that Harold Innis was among the first to recognize this transition, an "awareness of this major change in the social drama of this century" that led Innis to "shift his attention from economic history to the nature of communication past and present" (an interpretation of Innis's writings that McLuhan would reinforce with his essay "The Later Innis" [1953][18]).

16. See for example Karl Deutsch, "Higher Education and the Unity of Knowledge," in Lyman Bryson, Louis Finkelstein, and R. M. MacIver (Eds.), *Goals for American Education: 9th Symposium* (pp. 55–139), New York: Harper, 1950.

17. Carpenter et al., 1953: 1. The phrase comes from Karl Deutsch's essays "Mechanism, Organism, and Society: Some Models in Natural and Social Science" (1951a: 241) and "Mechanism, Teleology, and Mind" (1951b: 194), and is reiterated in his book *Nationalism and Social Communication* (1953 [1966]: 93), when he discusses cybernetic concepts of information, message transfer, and complementarity. This book would be part of the Culture and Communication Seminar library holdings.

18. Marshall McLuhan, 1953, "The Later Innis," *Queen's Quarterly* 60(3): 385–94.

Bateson and Ruesch's reflections on the position of the observer within the system of communication (a precursor to second-order cybernetics), and on open and closed networks of communication, are suggestive of the stance the Explorations group would take in the Ford proposal regarding their own critical outpost in Canada, enmeshed within North American and European indigenous and colonial histories. Innis, they argue, epitomized a uniquely Canadian observational post, "a bi-focal habit of vision" making natural to the outlook of Canadians "the historical and the scientific, the humanist and the technological simultaneously."[19] This outlook is represented in "the immediacy of Canadian reception of modern art and technology" by such artists as Scottish-born National Film Board of Canada animator Norman McLaren.[20] A transatlantic overlaying of historical events afforded Innis—and by extension their own research group—a "complex historical vision which is natural to those who think simultaneously of the attitudes and experience past and present, of French and British, English and North American." Innis interpreted the American Revolution as a cultural "clash between two networks of communication": the "closed" fur trades network controlled from France and England, which was "antithetic to settlement and the natural tendency to self-government" of the "open" social network of the United States. Canada remained within the closed fur trade network for a century after the United States had abandoned them. The authors believed this Canadian habit of vision offered an opportunity to understand the transition from a mechanized to an electrified media culture across the whole continent.[21]

In February 1951, McLuhan famously wrote to Innis categorically rejecting linear theories of information transmission: "Deutch's [*sic*] interesting pamphlet on communication is thoroughly divorced from any sense of the social functions performed by communication," he writes, further decrying the "fallacy of the Deutsch-Wiener approach" for "its failure to understand the techniques and functions of the traditional arts as the essential type of all human communication."[22] He then proposes an "experiment in communication" as a "means of linking a variety of specialized fields by what might

19. Carpenter et al., 1953: 1.

20. They also include Disney in this list of "Canadian pioneers of the new cinema medium", whose Canadian-born grandfather offered a perhaps more dubious national connection. Carpenter et al., 1953: 1.

21. Carpenter et al., 1953: 1.

22. Molinaro et al., 1987: 222.

be called a method of esthetic analysis of their common good. What I have been considering is a single mimeographed sheet to be sent out weekly or fortnightly to a few dozen people in different fields . . . illustrating the underlining unities of form which exist where diversity is all that meets the eye. Then, it is hoped there will be a feedback of related perception from various readers which will establish a continuous flow."[23] As he explained to Ezra Pound in the same period, the "object of [this] sheet is to open up intercommunication between several fields. To open up eyes and ears of people in physics, anthropology, history, etc. etc. to relevant developments in the arts."[24] But it is also here that we see the playfulness at stake in this project—the treatment of this "experiment" as itself a media art form that would, for all intents and purposes, develop into the *Explorations* project. For having just rejected the Deutsch-Wiener cybernetic approach in his letter to Innis, McLuhan would write to Wiener within weeks, stating, "As a friend and student of Sigfried Giedion's, I have paid special attention to your *Cybernetics* and *The Human Use of Human Beings*." Throughout this letter, McLuhan references the original 1950 issue of Wiener's *Human Use of Human Beings*, drawing a parallel between his just released *Mechanical Bride* and Wiener's comments on scientific discovery as the art of decoding the secrets of natural phenomena. And he concludes by suggesting that it is precisely an encounter with Karl Deutsch's "discussion of communication and education [that] led me to envisage an experiment in communication . . . I await certain feedback responses before proceeding."[25]

One such experiment from this period was to be called "NETWORK" and details the role of artists as essential circuits within the ever-increasing flux of messages: "The artist is at the centre of his network or milieu . . . By isolating and externalizing his inner drama . . . he offers the arrested means of contemplation of his time, an indispensable way of clarifying the ordinary imprecision and confusion of the endless crowd of messages circulating in the social network." It was, in essence, a second-order cybernetic model of communication study.

23. Molinaro et al., 1987: 223.

24. Molinaro et al., 1987: 218.

25. Marshall McLuhan to Norbert Wiener, 28 March 1951. File 135, Box 9, Norbert Wiener Papers, MIT Archives.

> The peculiar inside point of view in recent historiography, biography, photography, case histories, sociology, and anthropology is identical with the procedures of the physical sciences. Simultaneity and inclusiveness which characterize physics, painting, and poetry, in the twentieth century have always been implicit in the creative process in the arts and sciences. But current extension of self-awareness of techniques of apprehension and communication make practical a "reamalgamergence" of the domains of time and space, knowledge and power.[26]

Not surprisingly, the "Network" proposal concludes with the note, "Feedback: Karl Deutsch at MIT indicates serious work on communication involving Norbert Wiener, G. Kepes, and himself. Cf. books published under these names."[27]

McLuhan's "Network" experiment was arguably another step towards designing *Explorations* both as a serious scholarly publication project and a mosaic of ideas, a media art form in its own right. With Carpenter, McLuhan found a partner who shared the vision of an "experiment in communication," based on a commitment to intellectual exchange and bridging disciplines. Starting in 1951, they assembled the core team as well as a broader community of thinkers from across the arts, humanities, social and natural sciences to explore the effects of new media and technologies within contemporary culture. Especially coveted was Tyrwhitt's experience as a facilitator of research congresses with CIAM and her work with Giedion. As the proposal claims, "She had worked with him specifically on the problem of interdisciplinary study in the university and came to Toronto University especially to advance this kind of cooperation between departments of economics, political science, sociology, social work, anthropology, architecture, and town planning."[28]

"Well aware of the brilliant new developments in communication study at Massachusetts Institute of Technology," the Ford grant explains, gesturing both to Wiener's cybernetic conferences and to Claude Shannon and Warren Weaver's mathematical theory of communication, "the undersigned

26. LAC MG 31, D 156, 149, 4. See also McLuhan to Hugh Kenner, 30 January 1951. Box 46, Folder 2, Hugh Kenner Papers. Harry Ransom Humanities Research Center, University of Texas at Austin.

27. LAC MG 31, D 156, 149, 4.

28. Carpenter et al., 1953: 10.

propose to utilize these insights but to employ also the technique of studying the forms of communication, old and new, as art forms," an approach already "implicit in the very title of Harold Innis' *Bias of Communication*."[29] They proposed to study the effects of new media forms on patterns of language, economic values, social organization, individual and collective behaviour, always keeping in mind accompanying changes to the classroom and the networks of city life. In their eyes the central problem consisted of two aspects. First, "the creation of a new language of vision" that "arises from all our new visual media and which is part of the total language of modern culture." The notion of a new "language of vision" recalls in particular György Kepes's 1944 classic essay by the same title. *Language of Vision* proposed a radical revamping of art and design pedagogy in terms of visual communication, committed to identifying common patterns of unity across varied approaches to human experience. Kepes, a Hungarian-born professor of visual design at MIT associated with László Moholy-Nagy and the New Bauhaus, had in 1950 staged the exhibition "The New Landscape," a constellation of images of natural and scientific phenomena that attempted to shift our view from the static object to a method of pattern-seeing.[30] Jaqueline Tyrwhitt visited the exhibit while working with Giedion and most likely brought it to the attention of the Toronto faculty members. The group would publish an early draft of Kepes's introduction to his 1956 book *The New Landscape in Art and Science*. Kepes himself attempted to draw parallels between his project and cybernetics. In Wiener's own albeit hesitant contribution to the volume, he acknowledges that "the significance of the processes of breakdown is great not only in physics, but even in the study of sociological processes."[31] Second, the Toronto group proposed to study "the impact of this total social language on the traditional spoken and written forms of expression." These two core objectives they would pursue in the pages of *Explorations* through numerous contributions. As clearly indicated in an early draft of their Ford proposal, the core research group represented the five key disciplines that would supplement each other: anthropology, psychology, economics, town planning, and English.[32]

29. Carpenter et al., 1953: 4.

30. See Reinhold Martin, 2003, *The Organizational Complex: Architecture, Media, and Corporate Space*, Cambridge, MA: MIT Press, chapter 2: "Pattern-Seeing" (pp. 42–79).

31. Norbert Wiener, 1956, "Pure Patterns in a Natural World," in György Kepes (Ed.), *The New Landscape in Art and Science* (pp. 274–76), Chicago: P. Theobald. See also Martin, 2003: 38.

32. "Changing Patterns of Man and Society Associated with the New Media of

Exploring Interdisciplinarity

While no one discipline was privileged above the others, anthropology played a special role in creating a strong comparative framework from the start. In addition to anthropological discussions of cybernetics, the Sapir-Whorf theory was an important intellectual foundation. As with Innis, Edward Sapir (a German-born American who spent fifteen years in Ottawa working for the Geographical Survey of Canada) himself offered a multifocal habit of vision, working between linguistics, anthropology, and psychology. For the grant applicants, Sapir "brought together European attitudes towards psychoanalysis (emphasis on socially-situated personality) and North American attitudes towards social structure (culture)." Moreover, Sapir "fused the European concern with philology with [the] North American concern with dynamic patterns in language."[33] In the same way that Benjamin L. Whorf's metalinguistic techniques examined languages to understand collective strategies of adapting to changing notions of time and space, anthropological techniques for investigating cultural aspects of new media would complement psychological studies of personality. The anthropologist and ethnolinguist Dorothy Lee was arguably one of the group's "most influential force[s],"[34] contributing six articles on language, value, and perception. Her insight that peoples such as the Trobrianders perceived lineal order differently from Western cultures had already been cited by Bateson and Ruesch (1951), and was central to the delineation of acoustic and visual cultures undertaken by the Explorations group, and in later studies by both McLuhan and Carpenter.

Indeed, Carpenter's expansive understanding of anthropology was initially the driving force behind the publication. As McLuhan would write to Tyrwhitt in 1953, while she was in India developing a UN exhibition on low-cost housing, "Carpenter is keen to start a mag in connection with the project. So we are exploring possibilities."[35] In a letter to the Canadian Social Science Research Council, the authors explained that there was a shared desire to create a distinctly Canadian journal of anthropology. With the

Communication." Draft of Ford Foundation Proposal, likely 1953. LAC MG 31, D 156, 204, 26.

33. Carpenter et al., 1953: 2.

34. Carpenter, 2001: 240.

35. Marshall McLuhan to Jaqueline Tyrwhitt, 24 July 1953. Papers of Jaqueline Tyrwhitt.

Ford grant to "conduct a two-year interdisciplinary seminar, particularly in the fields of communications and anthropology, we felt our group might serve as the formal group to launch the desired journal." A "tentative outline" announced *Explorations* as a Canadian journal of communication and anthropology.[36] There was a need for a medium to bring articles together to "stimulate more and better articles, above all which will explore new fields, set trends, and communicate findings among that growing body of Canadians who are turning to anthropology and communications as new approaches to human relations."[37]

The meeting of anthropology and psychology, on the other hand, while perhaps electrifying, was also fraught with tensions. As Carpenter and McLuhan wrote in a joint article for the *Chicago Review* in 1956, entitled "The New Languages" (later extended and republished by Carpenter in *Explorations* 7), "the new mass media—film, radio, TV—are new languages, their grammars as yet unknown. Each codifies reality differently; each conceals a unique metaphysics."[38] Building on the insights drawn from anthropology that languages codify reality differently, Carpenter and McLuhan saw media as essentially codifying reality, space-time, in distinct ways. Perception and experience were central elements in the study of media as cultural forms, as particular forms of mediation. Carl Williams, the lone psychologist in the group, joined the project likely at the request of the University of Toronto's then vice president, Claude Bissell. As Carpenter recounted, Williams "sought to refine psychology to an objective science. It was for this reason he was invited to join our group. We felt we needed his bias to balance ours, and also to get Ford funding."[39] As is evident in looking at letters exchanged between Carpenter and McLuhan, a productive tension existed between the humanists and the scientists of the group that echoed divisions between critical communication studies and empirical mass communications research in the United States. The group's aim to create art-science collaborations was intended to create a novel kind of

36. LAC MG 31, D 156, 203, 30. See also Jana Mangold, 2014, "Zwischen Sprache/n: Explorationen der Medien zwischen Kultur und Kommunikation 1954," *Zeitscrhift für Medienwissenschaft* 11:155–62.

37. Letter addressed to the Canadian Social Science Research Council, likely mid-1953. LAC MG 31, D 156, 145, 41.

38. Edmund Carpenter and Marshall McLuhan, 1956, "The New Languages," *Chicago Review* 10(1): 46.

39. Carpenter, 2001: 241.

analytic framework whereby empirical facts could stand alongside poetic and humanistic rumination.

Nowhere was this more evident than in the media experiment undertaken by Carpenter and Williams. In developing their methodologies, seminar faculty and graduate students undertook a number of critical media experiments on changing patterns of perception resulting from new media. The CBC and the then Ryerson Institute placed studio space and media equipment at their disposal. The experiment tested their central hypothesis that different media (speech, print, radio, television) lend themselves to certain ideas and values.[40] With his graduate students, Williams undertook a systematic statistical analysis, later reporting in the *Canadian Journal of Psychology* that the results

> support the hypothesis that, under the conditions described, media do influence retention in terms both of immediate memory and of memory over a period of several months. The superior results of the television audience support the findings of previous experiments carried out before the advent of television [such as studies of media effects and persuasion by C. I. Hoveland and Joseph Klapper], that presentation of material by means of two sense modalities is more effective than either simple visual or aural presentation.[41]

Carpenter rejected such quantitative analysis. In a letter to group members of April 1955, he forcefully recounted that "my interest was media biases. I was convinced that the secret of TV was its extreme non-lineality, as opposed to the lineality of the book." The techniques proposed by the psychologists "stressed quantitative analyses and ignored the points I wished to investigate."[42] There is little doubt that both perspectives offered valid insights into the pedagogical experiences produced by different media. It is surprising that such findings have never been fully taken up by educational media researchers. Hopefully, the republication of these early studies will renew interest in the cognitive studies of media which have focussed too

40. Edmund Carpenter, 1954, "Certain Media Biases," *Explorations* 3:65–74; Carpenter and McLuhan, 1956; Edmund Carpenter, 1957, "The New Languages," *Explorations* 7:4–21.

41. D. C. Williams, J. Paul, and J. C. Ogilvie, 1957, "Mass Media, Learning, and Retention," *Canadian Journal of Psychology* 11(3): 162–63.

42. Edmund Carpenter to Explorations Group, April 1955. Papers of Jaqueline Tyrwhitt, TyJ\17\4.

narrowly, according to Carpenter and McLuhan, on attention and inputs and not enough on the creative and critical aspects of perception.

What is clear in reading through the *Explorations* issues is that Carpenter and McLuhan were most interested in the new kinds of learning made possible through the media. Carpenter and McLuhan would go one step further than Williams by asserting that the media are transforming the human sensorium. McLuhan, in particular, was influenced by research into human perception as part of his approach to media studies since he believed that these media were altering our senses, our forms of attention and knowledge production. This is why pedagogy is absolutely central to all of his books. In the acknowledgements page of *Understanding Media* (1964), McLuhan credits the National Association of Educational Broadcasters and U.S. Office of Education who in 1959–60 provided him with funding to produce his *Report on a Project in Understanding New Media*. This was a proposal for a radical high school curriculum centered around media. Many passages and ideas from this book are developed in *Understanding Media* and can be seen being developed in the pages of *Explorations*. As such, Carpenter and McLuhan are quite specific about the materiality of the media technologies, the "new languages" under discussion both in terms of their impact on the human sensorium and the environments they are creating. This would serve as the basis for a program of comparative and experimental media studies that each would pursue throughout his academic career.

Common Vocabularies

In the history of media studies in Canada and internationally, the *Explorations* journal is an important starting point for defining the research agenda of the so-called Toronto School. Yet, as Carpenter has later remarked, the school was not formal. Rather, comparing Toronto to an island, he described the group as "islanders simply watching a spectacular light show from afar. Toronto . . . housed a coterie of intellectuals and artists that would meet every day at four o'clock at the Royal Ontario Museum coffee shop: McLuhan, Tyrwhitt, Carpenter, Donald Theall, John Irving, students, sometimes Easterbrook and less often Innis, and often visitors Dorothy Lee, Sigfried Giedion, Ashley Montagu, Karl Polyani, and Roy Campbell."[43] Perhaps

43. Carpenter, 2001: 251

most worthy of recognition is the fact that the foundations of the Toronto School lie in the group's deep cross-disciplinary, international roots. These roots were largely transatlantic, but Carpenter's World War II experience in Japan and Tyrwhitt's work with CIAM and the United Nations in India brought an unusual range of experiences into their joint discussions.

The circulation and early reception of *Explorations* is difficult to trace, but indications are given in group members' correspondence and writings—though print runs typically totalled one thousand and circulation was international. As noted, *Explorations* was an experimental space, a project for which Carpenter himself was willing to gamble his own funds when the Ford funding was exhausted. In the April 1955 communication to the journal's coeditors, he wrote, "What is important is that we have ideas, not yet fully articulated, that are now exciting (already they're attracting considerable attention outside Toronto—the last three issues, Feb-Mar-Apr of *Scientific American* cite *Explorations* in reviews and article bibliographies). If we stop now, leaving the seminar incomplete, it will be just that—incomplete, which is good for neither staff nor students and will look as if we were in the thing only for the money."[44]

Ultimately, aside from McLuhan, the contributions of the group's other members to media theory have been largely overlooked. Carpenter contributed his cultural anthropological studies of visual media and indigenous cultures to the very shape that media studies would take during this period.[45] Tyrwhitt acted as liaison between the group and modernist architectural movements, providing vital links to members of Bauhaus, CIAM, and later the Athens-based World Society of Ekistics. She carried many of the group's insights to her professorship in Harvard's Graduate School of Design (1955–69) and later to her role as editor of the radical urban studies journal *Ekistics*, initiated in 1955 by Constantinos Doxiadis, who was developing a "science of human settlements."[46] Easterbrook became chair of the department of political economy at the University of Toronto (1961–70) and later copublished with seminar student Mel Watkins, a prominent

44. Edmund Carpenter to Explorations Group, April 1955. Papers of Jaqueline Tyrwhitt, TyJ\17\4.

45. See Harald Prins and John Bishop, 2002, "Edmund Carpenter: Explorations in Media & Anthropology," *Visual Anthropology Review* 17 (2): 110–40.

46. See Constantinos Doxiadis, 1968, *Ekistics: An Introduction to the Science of Human Settlements*, New York: Oxford University Press.

Canadian scholar and public intellectual. Williams became president of the University of Western Ontario (1967–77). Joan Rayfield joined Carpenter at Northridge, California, before returning to Toronto where she was a longtime professor of anthropology (York University). Donald Theall, one of the first graduate students, helped found the graduate programme in communication at Montreal's McGill University before assuming the presidency of Trent University. Many of the seminar's other students also went on to illustrious careers in fine arts, humanities, and sciences.

In 1953, the Explorations group posed a range of questions about the cultural implications of new media. "TV Wallops the Manuscript" was the conclusion: "the bout fought in the CBC studios"—a network, of course, created to foster a new sense of national unity in Canada by creating a mediated interpretation of the nation. TV's liveness was a catalyst for McLuhan and Carpenter to see electronic media as a return to orality, a new "acoustic space," and expressed a new aesthetics of freedom. And so, as the spoof cover of *Explorations* 2 also declared, the grammar of the movie and the TV screen promised to bring about the unity of arts that thinkers such as Giedion had long sought: "Unity is essential on the screen: it cannot be achieved by a production-line of specialists."[47] As McLuhan concluded in "Five Sovereign Fingers Taxed the Breath," included anonymously in *Explorations* 4,

> Telephone, gramophone, and RADIO are the mechanization of post-literate acoustic space. Radio returns us to the dark of the mind, to the invasions from Mars and Orson Welles; it mechanizes the well of loneliness that is acoustic space: the human heart-throb put on a PA system provides a well of loneliness in which anyone can drown.
>
> Movies and TV complete the cycle of mechanization of the human sensorium. With the omnipresent ear and the moving eye, we have abolished writing, the specialized acoustic-visual metaphor which established the dynamics of Western civilization. . . .
>
> NOBODY yet knows the language inherent in the new technological culture; we are all deaf-blind mutes in terms of the new situation. Our most impressive words and thoughts betray us by referring to the previously existent, not to the present.

47. See inside front cover of *Explorations* 2, April 1954.

> We are back in acoustic space. We begin again to structure the primordial feelings and emotions from which 3000 years of literacy divorced us.[48]

McLuhan and Carpenter's core ideas were captured perhaps most playfully in the final coedited issue, *Explorations* 8, devoted to the oral as an ode to James Joyce: "Verbi-Voco-Visual." The issue features seven essays, including one by McLuhan, that explore different aspects of oral culture—mostly concerned with a transition to a new orality. Twenty-four non-authored "Items," which include some previously published essays by McLuhan and Carpenter, appear as humorous intellectual sketches exploring topics like "Electronics as ESP," car commercials, bathroom acoustics, dictaphones, and of course wine. The final "Item," number 24, entitled "No Upside Down in Eskimo Art," reiterated McLuhan and Carpenter's core assertion that "after thousands of years of written processing of human experience, the instantaneous omnipresence of electronically processed information has hoicked us out of these age-old patterns into an auditory world." With the many rich new insights about new media cultures found in these eight coedited issues of *Explorations*, McLuhan, Carpenter, and their coeditors helped define a starting point for the emerging fields of media and communications studies.

References

Alfred Hallowell Papers. American Philosophical Society, Philadelphia.

Carpenter, Edmund S., Jaqueline Tyrwhitt, H. M. McLuhan, W. T. Easterbrook, and D. C. Williams. 1953. "University of Toronto: Changing Patterns of Language and Behavior and the New Media of Communication." Ford Foundation Archives. Grant File PA 53–70, Section 1, 1–11. Rockefeller Archive Center, New York.

Carpenter, Edmund. 1954. "Certain Media Biases." *Explorations* 3:65–74.

Carpenter, Edmund. 1957. "The New Languages." *Explorations* 7:4–21.

Carpenter, Edmund. 2001. "That Not-So-Silent Sea." In Donald Theall (Ed.), *The Virtual Marshall McLuhan* (pp. 236–61). Montreal: McGill-Queen's University Press.

Carpenter, Edmund, and Marshall McLuhan. 1956. "The New Languages." *Chicago Review* 10(1): 46–52.

Darroch, Michael. 2008. "Bridging Urban and Media Studies: Jaqueline Tyrwhitt and the *Explorations* Group, 1951–1957." *Canadian Journal of Communication* 33(2): 147–63.

48. "Five Sovereign Fingers Taxed the Breath." February 1955, *Explorations* 4:31–33.

Darroch, Michael. 2014. "Sigfried Giedion und die *Explorations*: Die anonyme Geschichte der Medienarchitektur," Johannes Passman (Trans.), *Zeitschrift für Medienwissenschaft* 11:144–54.

Darroch, Michael. 2016a. "Giedion and Explorations: Confluences of Space and Media in Toronto School Theorisation." In Norm Friesen (Ed.), *Transatlantic Developments in Media and Communication Studies* (pp. 62–87). Basel: Springer International.

Darroch, Michael. 2016b. "The Toronto School: Cross-Border Encounters, Interdisciplinary Entanglements." In David W. Park and Peter Simonson (Eds.), *The International History of Communication Studies* (pp. 276–301). New York: Routledge.

Darroch, Michael, and Janine Marchessault. 2009. "Anonymous History as Methodology: The Collaborations of Sigfried Giedion, Jaqueline Tyrwhitt and the Explorations Group 1953–1955." In Andreas Broeckmann and Gunalan Nadarajan (Eds.), *Place Studies in Art, Media, Science and Technology: Historical Investigations on the Sites and Migration of Knowledge* (pp. 9–27). Weimar: VDG.

Darroch, Michael, and Janine Marchessault. 2014. "Introduction: Urban Cartographies." In Michael Darroch and Janine Marchessault (Eds.), *Cartographies of Place: Navigating the Urban* (pp. 3–21). Montreal: McGill-Queen's University Press.

Deutsch, Karl. 1950. "Higher Education and the Unity of Knowledge." In Lyman Bryson, Louis Finkelstein, and R. M. MacIver (Eds.), *Goals for American Education: 9th Symposium* (pp. 55–139). New York: Harper.

Deutsch, Karl. 1951a. "Mechanism, Organism, and Society: Some Models in Natural and Social Science." *Philosophy of Science* 18(3): 230–52.

Deutsch, Karl. 1951b. "Mechanism, Teleology, and Mind." *Philosophy and Phenomenological Research* 12(2): 185–223.

Deutsch, Karl. 1953 [1966]. *Nationalism and Social Communication.* Cambridge, MA: MIT Press.

Doxiadis, Constantinos. 1968. *Ekistics: An Introduction to the Science of Human Settlements.* New York: Oxford University Press.

"Five Sovereign Fingers Taxed the Breath." February 1955. *Explorations* 4:31–33.

Ford Foundation. 1953. *Ford Foundation Annual Report 1953*. New York: Ford Foundation.

Ford Foundation Archives, Project Cards B-87, 1–6. New York: Rockefeller Archive Center.

Geiser, Reto. 2010. *Giedion in Between: A Study of Cultural Transfer and Transatlantic Exchange, 1938–1968.* Doctoral dissertation. ETH, Zurich.

Giedion, Sigfried. 1987. "A Faculty of Interrelations." In D. Huber (Ed.), *Wege in die Öffentlichkeit* (pp. 160–63). Zurich: Institut für Geschichte und Theorie der Architektur. [First published in 1943. *Michigan Society of Architects Weekly Bulletin* 1:1–4.]

Hugh Kenner Papers. Harry Ransom Humanities Research Center, University of Texas at Austin.

McLuhan, Marshall. 1953. "The Later Innis." *Queen's Quarterly* 60(3): 385–94.

McLuhan, Marshall. 1960. *Report on Project in Understanding New Media.* New York: National Association of Educational Broadcasters, Office of Education, U.S. Department of Health, Education and Welfare.

McLuhan, Marshall. 1964. *Understanding Media.* Toronto: McGraw-Hill.

Mangold, Jana. 2014. "Zwischen Sprache/n: Explorationen der Medien zwischen Kultur und Kommunikation 1954." *Zeitscrhift für Medienwissenschaft* 11:155–62.

Martin, Reinhold. 2003. *The Organizational Complex: Architecture, Media, and Corporate Space*. Cambridge, MA: MIT Press.
Molinaro, Matie, Corinne McLuhan, and William Toye. 1987. *Letters of Marshall McLuhan*. Toronto: Oxford University Press.
Norbert Wiener Papers, MIT Archives, Cambridge, MA.
Papers of Jaqueline Tyrwhitt (1885–1980). Royal Institute of British Architects, TYJ/16–18. RIBA British Architectural Library Drawings and Archives Collection, London.

Prins, Harald E. L., and John Bishop. 2002. "Edmund Carpenter: Explorations in Media & Anthropology." *Visual Anthropology Review* 17(2): 110–40.
Ruesch, Jurgen, and Gregory Bateson. 1951. *Communication, the Social Matrix of Psychiatry*. New York: Norton.
Shoshkes, Ellen. 2013. *Jaqueline Tyrwhitt: A Transnational Life in Urban Planning and Design*. Farnham, UK: Ashgate.
Theall, Donald. 1949. Review of *Cybernetics*, by Norbert Wiener. *Yale Scientific Magazine* 24(3): 4, 40, 42.
Theall, Donald. 1954. *Communication Theories in Modern Poetry: Yeats, Pound, Eliot and Joyce*. Doctoral dissertation. Toronto: University of Toronto.
Theall, Donald. 2001. *The Virtual Marshall McLuhan*. Montreal: McGill-Queen's University Press.
trans/formation: arts, communication, environment. 1950–52. Volumes 1–3. Harry Holtzman, ed. New York: Wittenborn, Schultz.
Vallye, Anna. 2009. "The Strategic Universality of *trans/formation*, 1950–1952." *Grey Room* 35:28–57.
Wiener, Norbert. 1948. *Cybernetics*. Cambridge, MA: MIT Press.
Wiener, Norbert. 1956. "Pure Patterns in a Natural World." In György Kepes (Ed.), *The New Landscape in Art and Science* (pp. 274–76). Chicago: P. Theobald.
Williams, D. C., J. Paul, and J. C. Ogilvie. 1957. "Mass Media, Learning, and Retention." *Canadian Journal of Psychology* 11(3): 157–63.

Research for this Introduction has been generously supported by the Social Sciences and Humanities Research Council of Canada through a Standard Research Grant and an Insight Grant, and through Dr. Darroch's 2015 Visiting Fellowship, Institute for Modern Languages Research, University of London. We are indebted to Dr. Kurt G. F. Helfrich, Chief Archivist and Collections Manager, Royal Institute of British Architects, British Architectural Library, and to Bethany J. Antos, Archivist at the Rockefeller Archive Center, as well as to the estates of Marshall McLuhan, Edmund Carpenter, and Jaqueline Tyrwhitt for their considerable support. Aspects of research on the history of *Explorations* have been published in Michael Darroch, 2008, "Bridging Urban and Media Studies: Jaqueline Tyrwhitt and the *Explorations* Group, 1951–1957," *Canadian Journal of Communication* 33: 147–69; Michael Darroch and Janine Marchessault, 2009, "Anonymous History as Methodology: The Collaborations of Sigfried Giedion, Jaqueline Tyrwhitt, and the *Explorations* Group (1951–55)," in Andreas Broeckmann and Gunalan Nadarajan (Eds.), *Place Studies in Art, Media, Science and Technology: Historical Investigations on the Sites and the Migration of Knowledge* (pp. 9–27), Weimar: VDG; Michael Darroch, 2014, "Sigfried Giedion und die *Explorations*: Die anonyme Geschichte der Medienarchitektur," translation by Johannes Passman, *Zeitschrift für Medienwissenschaft* 11:144–54; Michael Darroch and Janine Marchessault, 2014, "Introduction: Urban Cartographies," in Michael Darroch and Janine Marchessault (Eds.), *Cartographies of Place: Navigating the Urban* (pp. 3–21), Montreal: McGill-Queen's University Press; Michael Darroch, 2016a, "Giedion and Explorations: Confluences of Space and Media in Toronto School Theorisation," in Norm Friesen (Ed.), *Transatlantic Developments in Media and Communication Studies* (pp. 62–87), Basel: Springer International; Michael Darroch, 2016b, "The Toronto School: Cross-Border Encounters, Interdisciplinary Entanglements," in David W. Park and Peter Simonson (Eds.), *The International History of Communication Studies* (pp. 276–301), New York: Routledge.

Summaries of All Eight *Explorations* Volumes

Explorations 1

Explorations 1 took an audaciously new approach to communications and cultural research "cutting across" studies in anthropology, literature, social sciences, economics, folklore, and popular culture. From Copernican revolutions (Bidney) to a seventeenth-century translation of Sweden's Mohra witchcraft trials (Horneck); from senses of time (Leach) to the meaning of gongs (Carrington); from Majorcan customs (Graves) to a typography of functional analysis (Spiro); from Veblen's economic history (Riesman) to contemporary stress levels (Selye), the issue also included one of György Kepes's earliest drafts on fusing "art and science," an essay on Freud and vices (Goodman), and a return to childhood in Legman's work on comic books, before concluding with now classic essays by McLuhan and Frye. The cover of *Explorations* 1 depicts a series of masks from the award-winning film *The Loon's Necklace* (Crawley Films, 1948).

Explorations 2

Explorations 2's mischievous spoof covers, both front and back, inside and outside, were labelled "Feenicht's Playhouse," a reference to the Phoenix playhouse of Joyce's *Wake*. The key playful headline, "New Media Changing Temporal and Spatial Orientation to Self," was accompanied by multiple hoax articles, including "Time-Space Duality Goes" and "TV Wollops MS," a reference to television's apparent power over manuscript culture as evidenced by the group's media experiment at CBC studios. Exemplifying the playfulness of the core faculty's discussions about new media and behaviour, it is not surprising the McLuhan would publish in this issue his now famous article "Notes on the Media as Art Forms" alongside essays by other seminar participants: Tyrwhitt resuscitated an unpublished article, "Ideal Cities and the City Ideal," a historical survey of proposals for ideal urban designs (originally drafted for the defunct journal *trans/formation: art, communication, environment*). Carpenter's "Eternal Life" is a first analysis of Aivilik Inuit concepts of time; then student Donald Theall's "Here Comes Everybody" offered a snapshot of his research on Joyce and communication theories in modern poetry; anthropologist Dorothy Lee, who would visit the seminar in March 1955, offered a review of David Bidney's challenge to scholarly traditions in his 1953 book *Theoretical Anthropology*. In addition, Carpenter fleshed out the contents with contributions from political economy, anthropology, psychology, and English: the second part of Riesman's Veblen study; Lord Raglan on social classes; Derek Savage on "Jung, Alchemy and Self"; the *New Yorker*'s Stanley Hyman on Malraux's thesis of the "museum without walls"; and A. Irving Hallowell's extended essay on "Self and its Behavioral Environment"—the inspiration for the spoof cover.

Explorations 3

Explorations 3 was initially planned as a volume dedicated to Harold Innis. In the end, the issue would only include Innis's essay "Monopoly and Civilization," introduced by Easterbrook, and a series of reflections in "Innis and Communication" by seminar participants. In November 1954, the *Explorations* researchers attended the "Institute on Culture and Communication" organised by Ray Birdwhistell at the University of Louisville's Interdisciplinary Committee on Culture and Communication. A number of the contributions to *Explorations* 3 are essays or early drafts of contributions related to this conference (Birdwhistell, Lee, Trager & Hall). The issue also includes the initial, and substantially divergent, assessments of the group's first "media experiment" at CBC studios (April 1954) in the contributions by Carpenter and Williams. The issue is rounded out with an excerpt on reading and writing (Chaytor), a new translation of Kamo Chomei's *Hojoki* (Rowe & Kerrigan), a study of utopias (Wolfenstein), a reading of *Tristram Shandy* (MacLean), reflections on Soviet ethnography (Potekin & Levin), a reading of Shelley's hallucinations as narcissism and doublegoing (McCullough), a critical reassessment of the science of human behaviour (Wallace), and "Meat Packing and Processing," an anonymous entry, likely by McLuhan, alluding to Giedion's *Mechanization Takes Command* (1948). Like *Explorations* 1, the cover depicted an indigenous mask from the Northwest Coast also represented in the Crawley film *The Loon's Necklace* (1948).

Explorations 4

According to McLuhan, *Explorations* 4 was planned as an issue devoted to Sigfried Giedion. Published in February 1955, with a cover adapted from Kandinsky's *Comets* (1938), *Explorations* 4 was devoted to issues of space and placed a strong emphasis on modes of linguistic and poetic thought across multiple media. Poems by e. e. cummings and Jorge Luis Borges mingle with essays by seminar leaders McLuhan on "Space, Time, and Poetry," Carpenter on "Eskimo Poetry: Word Magic," Tyrwhitt on "The Moving Eye" (regarding comparative perceptual experiences of Western cities and the ancient Indian city of Fatehpur Sikri), and Williams on "auditory space"—a notion that "electrified" the group, as Carpenter later recounted. Northrop Frye and Stephen Gilman's essays on poetic traditions were juxtaposed with Millar MacLure and Marjorie Adix's odes to Dylan Thomas, who had died in 1953. Case studies by then graduate students Walter J. Ong on "Space in Renaissance Symbolism" and Joan Rayfield on "Implications of English Grammar" were aligned with Dorothy Lee's contribution on "Freedom, Spontaneity and Limit in American Linguistic Usage" and Lawrence Frank's early draft of "Tactile Communication." Both Lee and Frank had presented their contributions at Ray Birdwhistell's "Institute on Culture and Communication" in Louisville, in 1954. A "Media Log" and the now famous entry "Five Sovereign Fingers Taxed the Breath," both largely replicated from McLuhan's 1954 *Counterblast* pamphlet, were published anonymously. In addition to "Our Enchanted Lives," a memorandum of instructions for television programming adapted from a Procter & Gamble memo, "The Party Line" offered a second alleged memorandum "To All TIME INC. Bureaus and Stringers." An "Idea File" containing insights on oral, written, and technological cultural forms was culled from writings by Robert Graves, Edmund Leach, Walter Gropius, and E. T. Hall, among many others. With *Explorations* 4, the group revealed its commitment to the belief that communication studies was deeply rooted in anthropological and literary-poetic traditions, but equally informed by studies of mechanisation, technology, and culture.

Explorations 5

The cover of *Explorations* 5 returned to the playfulness of issue 2: the image of the famous Minoan "Our Lady of the Sports" figurine, held at the Royal Ontario Museum (the authenticity of which has long been disputed) was set in front of the *Toronto Daily Star*'s 8 April 1954 Home Edition front page, featuring the headline "H-Bomb in Mass Production, U.S." This juxtaposition between ancient artefact, contemporary media, and technological production set the stage for the issue: starting with Daisetz Suzuki's description of "Buddhist Symbolism", the issue follows with McLuhan's famous analysis of TV and radio in Joyce's *Finnegans Wake*. Such contrasts of new media forms continue with a "Portrait of James Joyce," an excerpt of a 1950 "Third Programme" BBC documentary edited by W. R. Rodgers, and the two-page "Anna Livia Plurabelle" section of Joyce's *Finnegans Wake*, set in experimental typography designed by Harley Parker and Toronto's Cooper and Beatty Ltd. The issue further juxtaposes essays by E. R. Leach on cultural conceptions of time and Jean Piaget on time-space conceptions of the child; anthropologists Claire Holt and Joan Rayfield on interpenetrations of language and culture and Carpenter's study of Eskimo space concepts; Rhodra Métraux on differences between the novel, play, and film versions of *The Caine Mutiny*; Roy Campbell on the fusion of oral and written traditions in the writings of Nigerian author Amos Tutuola, including an excerpt of his 1954 novel *My Life in the Bush of Ghosts*, and Harcourt Brown on Pascal; economist Kenneth Boulding on information theory and Easterbrook on economic approaches to communication; and an excerpt from Daniel Lerner and David Riesman's work on the modernisation of Turkey and the Middle East. Tyrwhitt and Williams contributed reflections on the seminar's second media experiment in "The City Unseen," an analysis of students' perceptions of the environment of the then Ryerson Institute. Anonymous entries included "Colour and Communication" and a transcription of satirist Jean Shepherd's radio broadcast "Channel Cat in the Middle Distance," likely courtesy of Carpenter. The issue is rounded out with a Letters File and an Ideas File, with contributions from E. R. Leach, Patrick Geddes, and Lawrence Frank.

Explorations 6

Writing to the Explorations Group in 1954, Carpenter worried about the funds from the Ford grant that were available for publishing this issue. *Explorations* 6 was funded through the sales of issue 5 and possibly Carpenter's own funds. The cover image for this issue was a section of *The Great Wave*, by Katsushika Hokusai. According to Carpenter's letter, this issue summarizes the group's "ideas and findings," which though "not fully articulated" were "new and exciting." He saw the issue as "a full seminar statement." Indeed, the issue brings together the interdisciplinary reflections and comparative media studies that characterized the group's methodology: a brilliant essay by radical anthropologist Dorothy Lee on "Wintu thought" (Lee would ultimately publish six essays in *Explorations* and had a significant influence on the seminar) and two essays on television that were solicited to reflect upon different geographical differences that shaped the experiences of the new medium—one in the US (Chayefsky) and the other the Soviet Union (Sharoyeva, the "top man" in the USSR television system). Also included were Giedion's classic essay on cave painting; a reflection on the phonograph alongside a consideration of "print's monopoly" by C. S. Lewis; as well as essays by McLuhan on media and events; language and magic (Maritain); writing and orality (Riesman); color (Parker); the evolution of the human mind (Montagu); and the anonymous entries "Print's Monopoly" and "Feet of Clay," likely drafted by McLuhan and Carpenter, which take up conflicts between old and new media environments. This issue contains the full spectrum of the weekly seminar's research undertakings over a two-year period.

Explorations 7

Explorations 7 (1957), the only issue without a table of contents, was edited by Carpenter and McLuhan solely and, with issue 8, sponsored by the *Toronto Telegram*. Easterbrook and Tyrwhitt were away, and Williams wanted his name taken off the masthead, allegedly because of the publication of American writer Gershon Legman's infamous "Bawdy Song . . . in Fact and in Print," a history of erotic writing. McLuhan had contributed to Legman's short-lived but hugely influential magazine *Neurotica* (1948–52), so the two had a previous connection. But the tension between Williams and the editors might have also been due to their different interpretations of the CBC/Ryerson media experiments which explored media sensory biases with a group of students discussed in issue 3 by Williams in scientific terms, and here again by Carpenter in his essay "The New Languages" in cultural terms. Carpenter argues that each medium (radio, TV, print) "codifies reality differently." To accompany this opening essay, they each included anonymous entries: the essay "Classroom Without Walls," later attributed to McLuhan, explores the ubiquitous mediasphere outside educational institutions, which teachers must begin to consider as an inherent and unavoidable pedagogical experience, followed by "Songs of the Pogo," a reference to the popular comic and LP of the period, which pervaded the McLuhan home. McLuhan saw relationships between "Jazz and Modern Letters," juxtaposed with Carpenter's reflections on the acoustic character of ancient and preliterate symbols, masks, and traditions in "Eternal Life of the Dream." Dorothy Lee contributed two essays to the issue on lineal and non-lineal codifications examined in the Trobriand language with responses by Robert Graves. The focus on educational matters also included a review of Riesman's *Variety and Constraint in American Education* as well as examinations of the cultural specificity of the Soviet press, Soviet novels, and Soviet responses to Elvis Presley. The particularity of an oral and noncapitalistic culture had been an important point of comparison for the Explorations Group, especially Carpenter and McLuhan. Harley Parker designed the issue's cover.

Explorations 8

Explorations 8 (1957) is perhaps the most famous of all the issues. It was devoted to the oral—"Verbi-Voco-Visual"—and was edited primarily by McLuhan and again published by the *Toronto Telegram* and the University of Toronto. The issue was filled with visual experimentation; framed by extensive play with typography in the spirit of the Vorticists and for the first time the extensive use of "flexitype" by Harley Parker, then display designer at the ROM. Seen throughout are Parker's experiments with typography as well as color printing, the first time in the history of the journal. A photomontage from László Moholy-Nagy's *Vision in Motion* (1947) depicting a man's face with an ear juxtaposed over an eye is the frontispiece to the issue. The issue features seven essays, including one by McLuhan, that explore different aspects of oral culture—mostly concerned with a transition to a new orality. Twenty-four non-authored "Items," which include some previously published essays by McLuhan and Carpenter, appear as humorous intellectual sketches exploring topics like "Electronics as ESP," car commercials, bathroom acoustics, dictaphones, and of course wine. The final "Item," number 24, entitled "No Upside Down in Eskimo Art," reiterated McLuhan and Carpenter's core assertion that "after thousands of years of written processing of human experience, the instantaneous omnipresence of electronically processed information has hoicked us out of these age-old patterns into an auditory world."

Michael Darroch (University of Windsor)
Janine Marchessault (York University)
2016

VOLUME 1

SIX COPERNICAN REVOLUTIONS

Ever since the publication in 1543 of the *Six Books Concerning the Revolution of the Heavenly Spheres* by Nicholas Copernicus philosophers and scientists have tended to hail every major innovation in modern thought as a kind of 'Copernican revolution'. Thus, in the 18th century Immanuel Kant regarded his *Critique of Pure Reason* as marking a Copernican revolution in the sphere of the philosophy of science and in the 20th century A. L. Kroeber refers to the ethnological theory of 'the superorganic' as another Copernican revolution in scientific thought. I propose in this paper to examine briefly six such 'Copernican revolutions' and to indicate how each of these has affected the orientation and perspective of modern thought. The basis of my selection is the assumption that in each of the examples chosen a theory has been put forward which goes counter to obvious appearances and to the generally accepted logic of common sense. The six Copernican revolutions which I have selected refer to the revolution in astronomy by Nicholas Copernicus, the revolution in metaphysics and morals by Baruch Spinoza, the revolution in the philosophy of science by Immanuel Kant, the sociological revolution by Auguste Comte, the ethnological revolution initiated by Edward B. Tylor and his followers in Germany, Britain and America, and finally, the linguistic revolution proposed by modern semanticists and ethnolinguists.

The revolution in astronomy initiated by Nicholas Copernicus is too well known to require lengthy elaboration. Briefly, the Copernican theory introduced a heliocentric perspective instead of the geocentric perspective of Aristotle and Ptolemy. By assuming that the sun rather than the earth was the centre of our universe and by attributing motion to the earth rather than to the sun, Copernicus, following suggestions by the Greek astronomer Aristarchus, went counter to the commonly accepted philosophical and religious thought of his time as well as to the obvious beliefs of common sense. While Copernicus himself continued to adhere to the Greek and Hebrew-Christian notion of a finite universe limited by the sphere of the fixed stars, his followers, notably the philosophers Giordano Bruno and René Descartes, inferred from his theory the idea of an infinite universe in which our solar system was but one among many. Through the work of Galileo Galilei, John Kepler and Isaac Newton's theory of universal gravitation, the Copernican theory became established in modern scientific thought.

In the 17th century, the philosopher Baruch Spinoza was the first to develop systematically the implications of the Copernican revolution in astronomy for metaphysics and morals. Spinoza's *Ethics* and *Tractatus Theologico-Politicus* may be viewed as attempts to break away from the traditional, authoritarian religion and ethics and to extend the revolution initiated in astronomy and physics by Copernicus and Galilei to the sphere of metaphysics, psychology, and ethics. This he did by introducing a naturalistic and religious philosophical anthropology which precluded dogmatic beliefs in supernatural phenomena and in an anthropomorphic deity. He conceived of man as part of the order of nature and not as a special creation not subject to the universal laws of nature. God was conceived by him as the dynamic principle of order immanent within nature as a whole *(natura naturans)* in opposition to the traditional notion of God as the transcendent creator of the order of nature. As the dynamic principle of order within nature, the God of Spinoza was essentially the impersonal God of the scientist, a God of Truth who may be the object of intellectual love but who, unlike the God of the Patriarchs and of the Christian church, did not reciprocate man's love and had no special concern for human welfare and wishful thinking. Spinoza's attempt to conceive all things through God or nature may be interpreted as a 'Copernican revolution' whereby all levels of natural phenomena are conceived from the perspective of an infinite being rather than from the finite, anthropocentric perspective of man.

Building upon Descartes' dualistic theory of the relation of body and mind, Spinoza originated the theory of the parallelism of body and mind and asserted that mind like body is subject to determinate laws of activity, thereby providing a basic postulate of modern psychology. He considered the mind as a 'spiritual automaton' subject to laws of its own, just as the body was subject to the laws of motion described by Galilei. Furthermore, Spinoza was among the first of the Renaissance philosophers to apply the Galilean law of inertia to psychology and ethics by postulating that every form of life endeavours by nature to persevere in existence indefinitely unless hindered from doing so by some superior force. The idea of the primacy of the *conatus* for self-preservation — later developed independently by Charles Darwin from an evolutionary point of view — marked a complete departure from the theory of the Western theologians who held that all forms of nature were directed toward fixed ends or final causes and that human nature existed for the sake of some transcendental, supernatural end. Furthermore, in his *Ethics* Spinoza endeavoured to construct a psychology of the emotions in which the emotions were considered as dynamic forces subject to laws. The notion that there is a logic of the emotions and that the emotions are not merely irrational forces or diseases which have to be suppressed is one that was scarcely appreciated in his time and is but now, since the advent of modern psychiatry, beginning to be recognized.

In moral theory, Spinoza's revolutionary thought was expressed in his transvaluation of traditional moral values — a point which Friedrich Nietzsche later recognized — and by his reinterpretation of human virtue in terms of the efficient power of the individual. His moral theory was naturalistic and this-worldly and was opposed to the religious view that life on earth is but a preparation for life-after-death. Not grief and a sense of sin or guilt for vicarious crimes but joy and peace of mind are the leading motifs of his philosophy of life. Throughout his psychology and ethics one finds the underlying theme that human nature, like nature as a whole, must first be understood and obeyed before it may be commanded and controlled. Spinoza's philosophy is the classic attempt of modern times to construct a rational, universal system of human salvation which may dispense with supernatural sanctions and precludes special historical revelations through chosen peoples or individuals.

The self-styled Copernican revolution of Immanuel Kant is, in spirit, the antithesis of Spinoza's. Whereas Spinoza endeavored to transcend a purely anthropocentric perspective by conceiving all things through God or infinite nature, Kant, by contrast, may be said to have reinstated the anthropocentric approach. As Etienne Gilson has stated in *The Spirit of Medieval Philosophy* (p. 245): 'The sun that Kant set at the centre of the world was man himself, so that his revolution was the reverse of the Copernican and led to an anthropocentrism a good deal more radical, though radical in another fashion, than any of which the Middle Age is accused.' By making man's 'transcendental ego' the measure of all things, Kant reversed the classic metaphysical approach of Plato and Aristotle. Kant's *Critiques* were, in effect, critical, anthropological treatises which investigated the *a priori* conditions of natural science and ethics as given cultural disciplines, although Kant himself did not clearly recognize this point as regards his *Critique of Pure Reason.*

4 Kant, as is well known, accepted the validity of Newtonian science and sought for the conditions in the human understanding which made mathematics and natural science in general possible and intelligible. His 'answer' to Hume was that theoretical, pure reason was limited by its *a priori* categorial structure to the cognition and organization of phenomena and hence, in fundamental agreement with David Hume, he denied the possibility of an ontological knowledge of nature. He did not, however, entirely exclude the concept of a metaphysical or noumenal reality, but maintained that 'things-in-themselves' were not the object of scientific knowledge. According to Kant, 'the understanding does not derive its laws *(a priori)* from, but prescribes them to, nature.' This meant, in the final analysis, that Kant tended to reduce natural philosophy and theoretical science to anthropology — a thesis which historians of philosophy have been slow in recognizing.

Just as Kant began his critique of scientific knowledge by accepting the fact of mathematical science, so, as Ernst Cassirer has observed, he began his ethics and his *Anthropologie* by accepting the fact of civilization. Unlike Rousseau, Kant did not begin with 'the natural man' in order to arrive at an understanding of human culture, but, beginning with civilized man and accepting the reality of historical cultural achievements, he proceeded to outline the necessary conditions which would enable man to attain an ideal, moral perfection and a rational state of society.

There is, for Kant, a fundamental difference between the object or sphere of theoretical understanding and of practical reason. Nature is the sphere of mathematical, scientific law. There is an isomorphic relation between the phenomena of nature and the human understanding, such that the universal laws of nature are identical with the synthetic *a priori* rules of the understanding. Human practical reason, on the other hand, is not limited by any *a priori* categories which may determine the conditions of its experience; it is completely free and undetermined. Hence practical reason is governed by its own categorical imperative and can postulate what man ought to believe concerning such noumenal entities as God and the human soul. So far as moral culture is concerned, the maxim 'thou canst because thou oughtest', holds good; whereas in the sphere of natural science man is confronted with a necessary order of phenomena which is not subject to the human will. This explains why Kant did not postulate any categorial structure of practical reason, since to have done so would have meant a denial of man's moral freedom and autonomy. Man does not create the order of nature of which he is a part, although the human understanding through its categories does predetermine the general modes through which it is perceived. Man does, however, postulate his own moral laws and ideals and freely sets up moral standards for all mankind. In short, natural phenomena are given in experience, but moral phenomena have to be willed into existence in accordance with the dictates of practical reason and the human conscience.

While Kant postulated that man was morally free and capable of legislating for himself in obedience to the categorical imperative, he thought, nevertheless, that social phenomena could be interpreted 'as if' they were subject to natural laws of their own. Kant thought that it would take the equivalent of a Kepler and a Newton to figure out and explain the end, or plan, of nature in the progressive development of the original endowments of the entire human species in the course of history, and he himself did not feel equal to the task. He modestly suggested in his 'Idea for a Universal History with Cosmopolitan Intent' the regulative idea by means of which the historian may look at human history 'as if' it were a process determined according to some law or plan of nature. In the 19th century, Auguste Comte attempted to construct such a scientific philosophy of history as Kant had envisaged.

In contrast to the 17th and 18th century metaphysical rationalism, the keynote of 19th century philosophical thought is history. Even those who accepted the critical, anthropological idealism of Kant felt that the Kantian approach had to be expanded so as to provide a logical and epistemological analysis of the conditions of historical, cultural thought.

The Copernican revolution brought about by Auguste Comte consists in his thesis that man is by nature a social, historical animal whose mentality and thought is subject to natural laws of historical development. As against the classical, metaphysical approach of the philosophical anthropologists of the 18th century, Comte maintained that man was to be known through a study of historical humanity, not humanity through a study of universal human nature. Comte, it should be noted, posited a theory of psychocultural evolution through fixed stages but still adhered to a nonevolutionary theory of the fixity of species in the realm of biology.

Comte's distinction as the founder of the science of sociology lies in his discernment that social phenomena constitute a distinct level supervening upon biological phenomena. He conceived sociology as a kind of 'social physics' subject to laws of its own. His famous law of the three stages in the development of society (reminiscent of Hegel), from the theological, through the metaphysical, to the positive, was taken by him to establish the new science of sociology upon a sure foundation of positive fact. Henceforth human history in its social and intellectual aspects was to be understood as a natural science as well as a normative science which defined the inevitable goal of the progress of humanity. Following Condorcet, Comte conceived of humanity as a single individual subject to development in time, with the most advanced societies representing humanity at a given historical period. Comte's philosophy of history presupposed a fixed, closed system in that the positive, scientific stage represented the ultimate goal of development. This point was early detected by his more critical followers who, like Emile Durkheim, thought that it was arbitrary to consider the third stage as the final and definitive stage of humanity.

Thus, for Comte, the Greek maxim 'know thyself' came to mean 'know thyself as a product of historical humanity.' This historical thesis was soon converted by later thinkers, such as Friedrich Nietzsche and Karl Marx, into a radical societal determinism and social relativism. Once society was understood as a reality *sui generis,* and individual mentality as but a function or product of social institutions, then it followed logically, as Nietzsche discerned so clearly, that a complete transvaluation of moral values was in order. Contrary to the Kantian doctrine, the ideal of a categorical imperative having universal objective validity for all mankind was dismissed as a delusion of the idealists and the values of good and evil were evaluated as expression of class structure. The historical materialism of Karl Marx is but a special variation of this sociological relativism.

Somewhat later, but parallel to Comtean sociology, modern ethnology was originated with the publication of Edward B. Tylor's *Primitive Culture.* Ethnology, like sociology, was at first understood as the study of culture history and of the achievements and acquired capabilities of man as a member of society. This meant in practice that the ethnologist was concerned with the historical and comparative study of the impersonal achievements or products of man in society, whereas the sociologist sought to determine the nature and modes of social organization and social processes. For the ethnologist what mattered most was the objective evidence, the traditions, customs and artifacts which comprised the capital of cultural productivity; he was not concerned to demonstrate, as was the sociologist, the primacy of society and of 'social facts' in determining the behaviour and thought of the individual, but rather to indicate the historical sequence and evolutionary stages in the historical development of culture.

In time, however, as may be seen from A. L. Kroeber's classic paper on 'The Superorganic', culture, too, was conceived as a reality *sui generis*. All that the sociologists, such as Emile Durkheim, had claimed in behalf of society, the ethnologists now claimed in the name of culture. Culturology, rather than sociology, it was now held, ought to be recognized as the most universal science of man and to it alone pertained the integrating function of synthesizing all the human sciences. Such recent volumes as *The Science of Man in the World Crisis* edited by Ralph Linton and Leslie A. White's *The Science of Culture* have articulated this universal claim most clearly. Thus, instead of sociological determinism and relativism there arose the doctrine of cultural determinism and relativism. Instead of the doctrine that society makes man, the thesis was now proposed that culture makes man as well as society. The ethnological Copernican revolution was all set to supersede the sociological revolution.

From a philosophical perspective, it is of interest to note that modern historical culturology and Neo-Kantian historical idealism have much in common. Both approaches stress the primacy of symbolism and the phenomenological reality of culture forms. According to Ernst Cassirer's position, man cannot know himself except through an analysis of the symbolic expressions of historical culture. Man is said to be an 'animal symbolicum' rather than an 'animal rationale' in the Aristotelian sense. Thus, both the ethnological positivists and the Neo-Kantian idealists tend to reduce the category of nature to culture; reality as known has become a function of culture. On this premise, as Melville Herskovits has argued in his *Man and His Works,* cultural relativism in the field of moral values is a logical consequence.

And now, it appears, the 'metalinguists' have put forth a new claim to a Copernican revolution of their own which threatens to supersede that of the culturologists. Neither culture nor society, they tend to maintain, but language is the ultimate and primary determinant of human thought. Philosophical and literary semanticists deriving from Alfred Korzybski and ethnolinguists inspired by Benjamin Lee Whorf have joined forces to proclaim anew the primacy of the Word, but in a sense of which the Christian theologians never dreamed. Once more, the metalinguists derive indirect moral support from the Neo-Kantian philosophy of language, as developed by Cassirer and Wilbur Marshall Urban, which regards the symbolic forms of language as *organs* of reality, as instruments by whose agency anything real becomes an object for intellectual apprehension. Contemporary ethnolinguists, such as Henry Lee Smith and George L. Trager, are, however, more concerned to demonstrate the thesis of ethnolinguistic relativism by showing how the categories of a given language determine the cultural perspective and behavioural orientation of its adherents. 'For each society,' they claim, 'the total culture and all its subdivisions must be analyzed as closed systems, having no necessary resemblance to, or connection with, those of any other society.' Each ethnolinguistic world is thought of as a monadic, closed, self-regulating system and the dream of philosophers and scientists of a common world of mutual, transcultural intelligibility appears to be excluded on principle. The gospel of linguistic determinism and relativism has replaced that of cultural determinism and relativism.

In conclusion, I am inclined to the view that the only one of the Copernican revolutions which has proved an unqualified success has been the original one of Copernicus in astronomy. As I have demonstrated in my study of *The Psychology and Ethics of Spinoza*, the metaphysical and moral revolution of Spinoza is only partially valid. While his naturalism and humanism have continued to influence eminent men of letters, scholars and scientists down to the present, his proposed metaphysical and methodological revolution whereby man was to conceive all things from the perspective of God or infinite nature has proved delusory. Instead, modern scholars have recognized for the most part the large element of truth contained in the Kantian critical revolution, namely, that the human mind is not a mere passive receptacle of what is 'given' to it by nature but that it also contributes its own constructs in the epistemological process. Man, in other words, cannot transcend himself and all his experiences are, in the last analysis, peculiarly human experiences determined by his own psychophysical nature and potentialities. There is no point in trying to divest ourselves of our common humanity; one only succeeds in being either ridiculous or bestial by trying to do so.

On the other hand, the sociological, culturological and ethnolinguistic revolutions, which still have many and powerful adherents, appear, to me at least, to be extreme positions each containing an important element of truth. As indicated in my *Theoretical Anthropology*, what I find objectionable in each instance is the radical determinism and relativism which their more ardent adherents advocate. In order to extend the domain and frontiers of natural science to the human sphere, dogmatic sociologists, culturologists and linguists have tended to maintain a position of rigid determinism which leaves no scope for human initiative and self-determination — as if it were the function of science to invent laws where none exist. Thus, the so-called human sciences have become dehumanized to the extent that man, their author and creator, seems to have been excluded from any significant role in determining for himself the goals and values by which, and for which, he must live. An adequate science and philosophy of man, it seems to me, must be one that reckons seriously with man himself as a factor engendering new culture forms and values. This implies that the social scientist must not exclude man himself as a self-determining agent, while analyzing the empirical, historical and sociocultural factors which affect his conduct individually and collectively. The humanistic scholar, in turn, must consider man as a part of the order of nature and of culture and not look upon him as if he were a law unto himself and not subject to the laws of nature and the regularities of culture. The greatest danger to the humanistic scholar and to the social scientist lies in their mutual, dogmatic assertion of their unqualified, precious autonomy.

David Bidney

CRONUS AND CHRONOS

My starting point in this essay is simply *time* as a word in the English language. It is a word which we use in a wide variety of contexts and it has a considerable number of synonyms, yet is oddly difficult to translate. In an English-French dictionary *time* has one of the longest entries in the book; time is *temps,* and *fois,* and *heure,* and *âge,* and *siècle,* and *saison* and lots more besides, and none of these are simple equivalents; *temps* perhaps is closest to English *time,* but *beau temps* is not a 'lovely time'!

Outside of Europe this sort of ambiguity is even more marked. For example, the language of the Kachin people of North Burma seems to contain no single word which corresponds at all closely to English *time*; instead there are numerous partial equivalents. For example, in the following expressions the Kachin equivalent of the word *time* would differ in every case:

	Kachin word for time
The *time* by the clock is - - - - - - - -	*ahkying*
A long *time* - - - - - - - - - - - - -	*na*
A short *time* - - - - - - - - - - - - -	*tawng*
The present *time* - - - - - - - - - - -	*ten*
Spring *time* - - - - - - - - - - - - -	*ta*
The *time* has come - - - - - - - - - - -	*hkra*
In the *time* of Queen Victoria - - - - - -	*lakhtak, aprat*
At any *time* of life - - - - - - - - - - -	*asak*

and that certainly does not exhaust the list. I do not think a Kachin would regard these words as in any way synonyms for one another.

This sort of thing suggests an interesting problem which is quite distinct from the purely philosophical issue as to what is the *nature* of Time. This is: How do we come to have such a verbal category as *time* at all? How does it link up with our everyday experiences?

Of course in our own case, equipped as we are with clocks and radios and astronomical observatories, time is a given factor in our social situation; it is an essential part of our lives which we take for granted. But suppose we had no clocks and no scientific astronomy, how then should we think about time? What obvious attributes would time then seem to possess?

Perhaps it is impossible to answer such a very hypothetical question, and yet, clocks apart, it seems to me that our modern English notion of time embraces at least two different kinds of experience which are logically distinct and even contradictory.

Firstly, there is the notion of repetition. Whenever we think about measuring time we concern ourselves with some kind of metronome; it may be the ticking of a clock or a pulse beat or the recurrence of days or moons or annual seasons, but always there is something which repeats.

Secondly, there is the notion of non-repetition. We are aware that all living things are born, grow old and die, and that this is an irreversible process.

I am inclined to think that all other aspects of time, duration for example or historical sequence, are fairly simple derivatives from these two basic experiences:

(a) that certain phenomena of nature repeat themselves
(b) that life change is irreversible.

Now our modern sophisticated view tends to throw the emphasis on the second of these aspects of time. 'Time', says Whitehead, 'is sheer succession of epochal durations'[1]: it goes on and on. All the same we need to recognize that this irreversibility of time is psychologically very unpleasant. Indeed, throughout the world, religious dogmas are largely concerned with denying the final 'truth' of this common sense experience.

Religions of course vary greatly in the manner by which they purport to repudiate the 'reality' of death; one of the commonest devices is simply

[1] A. N. Whitehead, *Science and the Modern World*, 1927, p. 158.

to assert that death and birth are the same thing — that birth follows death, just as death follows birth. This seems to amount to denying the second aspect of time by equating it with the first.

I would go further. It seems to me that if it were not for religion we should not attempt to embrace the two aspects of time under one category at all. Repetitive and non-repetitive events are not, after all, logically the same. We treat them both as aspects of 'one thing', time, not because it is rational to do so, but because of religious prejudice. The idea of Time, like the idea of God, is one of those categories which we find necessary because we are social animals rather than because of anything empirical in our objective experience of the world.[1]

Or put it this way: In our conventional way of thinking, every interval of time is marked by repetition; it has a beginning and an end which are 'the same thing' — the tick of a clock, sunrise, the new moon, New Year's day . . . but every interval of time is only a section of some larger interval of time which likewise begins and ends in repetition . . . so, if we think in this way, we must end by supposing that 'Time itself' (whatever that is) must repeat itself. Empirically this seems to be the case. People *do* tend to think of time as something which ultimately repeats itself; this applies equally to Australian aborigines, Ancient Greeks, and modern mathematical astronomers.[2] My view is that we think this way not because there is no other possible way of thinking, but because we have a psychological (and hence religious) repugnance to contemplating either the idea of death or the idea of the end of the universe.

I believe this argument may serve to throw some light upon the representation of time in primitive ritual and mythology. We ourselves, in thinking about time, are far too closely tied to the formulations of the astronomers; if we do not refer to time as if it were a coordinate straight line stretching from an infinite past to an infinite future, we describe it as a circle or cycle. These are purely geometrical metaphors, yet there is nothing intrinsically geometrical about time as we actually experience it. Only mathematicians are ordinarily inclined to think of repetition as an aspect of motion in a circle. In a primitive, unsophisticated community the metaphors of repetition are likely to be of a much more homely nature: vomiting, for example, or the oscillations of a weaver's shuttle, or the sequence of agricultural activities, or even the ritual exchanges of a series of interlinked marriages. When we describe such sequences as 'cyclic'

[1] *Année Sociologique*, 5:248; also H. Hubert and M. Mauss, 'Etude sommaire de la representation du temps dans la religion et la magie.' in *Melanges d'histoire des religions*, 1909.
[2] e.g. Fred Hoyle, *The Nature of the Universe*, 1950, p. 108.

we innocently introduce a geometrical notation which may well be entirely absent in the thinking of the people concerned.

Indeed in some primitive societies it would seem that the time process is not experienced as a 'succession of epochal durations' at all; there is no sense of going on and on in the same direction, or round and round the same wheel. On the contrary, time is experienced as something discontinuous, a repetition of repeated reversal, a sequence of oscillations between polar opposites: night and day, winter and summer, drought and flood, age and youth, life and death. In such a scheme the past has no 'depth' to it, all past is equally past; it is simply the opposite of now.

It is religion, not common sense, that persuades men to include such various oppositions under a single category such as *time*. Night and day, life and death are logically similar pairs only in the sense that they are both pairs of contraries. It is religion that identifies them, tricking us into thinking of death as the night time of life and so persuading us that non-repetitive events are really repetitive.

The notion that the time process is an oscillation between opposites — between day and night or between life and death — implies the existence of a third entity — the 'thing' that oscillates, the 'I' that is at one moment in the daylight and at another in the dark, the 'soul' that is at one moment in the living body and at another in the tomb. In this version of animistic thinking the body and the grave are simply alternative temporary residences for the life-essence, the soul. Plato, in the *Phaedo,* actually uses this metaphor explicitly: he refers to the human body as the *tomb* of the soul (psyche). In death the soul goes from this world to the underworld; in birth it comes back from the underworld to this world.

This is of course a very common idea both in primitive and less primitive religious thinking. The point that I want to stress is that this type of animism involves a particular conception of the nature of time and, because of this, the mythology which justifies a belief in reincarnation is also, from another angle, a mythological representation of 'time itself'. In the rest of this essay I shall attempt to illustrate this argument by reference to familiar material from classical Greece.

At first sight it may appear that I am arguing in a circle. I started by asking what sort of concrete real experience lies at the back of our abstract notion of time. All I seem to have done so far is to switch from the oscillations of abstract time to the oscillations of a still more abstract concept, soul. Surely that is worse than ever. For us perhaps, yes. We can 'see' time on a clock; we cannot see people's souls; for us, souls are more abstract than time. But for the Greeks, who had no clocks, time was a total abstraction, whereas the soul was thought of as a material substance consisting of the marrow of the spine and the head, and forming a sort of concentrated essence of male semen. At death, when the body was placed in the tomb this marrow coagulated into a live snake. In Greek ancestor cults the marked emphasis on snake worship was a not a residue of totemism: it was simply that the hero-ancestor in

his chthonic form was thought to be an actual snake.[1] So for the Greeks, of the pre-Socratic period anyway, the oscillation of the soul between life and death was quite materially conceived — the soul was either material bone-marrow (in the living body) or it was a material snake (in the tomb).

If then, as I have suggested, the Greeks conceived the oscillations of time by analogy with the oscillations of the soul, they were using a concrete metaphor. Basically it is the metaphor of sexual coitus, of the ebb and flow of the sexual essence between sky and earth (with the rain as semen), between this world and the underworld (with marrow-fat and vegetable seeds as semen), between man and woman. In short, it is the sexual act itself which provides the primary image of time. In the act of copulation the male imparts a bit of his life-soul to the female; in giving birth she yields it forth again. Coitus is here seen as a kind of dying for the male; giving birth as a kind of dying for the female. Odd though this symbolism may appear, it is entirely in accord with the findings of psycho-analysts who have approached the matter from quite a different point of view.[2]

All this I suggest throws light upon one of the most puzzling characters in classical Greek mythology, that of Cronus, father of Zeus. [Aristotle] declared that Cronus (Kronos) was a symbolical representation of Chronos, Eternal Time,[3] — and it is apparently this association which has provided our venerable Father Time with his scythe. Etymologically, however, there is no close connection between *kronos* and *chronos*, and it seems unlikely that [Aristotle] should have made a bad pun the basis for a major issue of theology, though this seems to be the explanation generally put forward. Whatever may have been the history of the Cronus cult — and of that we know nothing — the fact that at one period Cronus was regarded as a symbol for Time must surely imply that there was something about the mythological character of Cronus which seemed appropriate to that of a personified Time. Yet it is difficult for us to understand this. To us Cronus appears an entirely disreputable character with no obvious temporal affinities.

Let me summarize briefly the stories which relate to him:

---

1 R. B. Onians, *Origins of European Thought,* 1951; Jane Harrison, *Prolegomena to the Study of Greek Religion* (3rd edn), 1922.
2 Geza Roheim, *Animism, Magic and the Divine King,* 1930, pp. 20-26.
3 [Aristotle], *de Mundo,* ch. 7.

1. Cronus, King of the Titans, was the son of Uranus (sky) and Ge (earth). As the children of Uranus were born, Uranus pushed them back again into the body of Ge. Ge to escape this prolonged pregnancy armed Cronus with a sickle with which he castrated his father. The blood from the bleeding phallus fell into the sea and from the foam was born Aphrodite (universal fecundity).

2. Cronus begat children by his sister Rhea. As they were born he swallowed them. When the youngest, Zeus, was born, Rhea deceived Cronus by giving him a (phallic) stone wrapped in a cloth instead of the new-born infant. Cronus swallowed the stone instead of the child. Zeus thus grew up. When Zeus was adult, Cronus vomited up his swallowed children, namely: Hades, Poseidon, Hestia, Hera, Demeter, and also the stone phallus, which last became a cult object at Delphi. Zeus now rebelled against King Cronus and overthrew him; according to one version he castrated him. Placed in restraint, Cronus became nevertheless the beneficent ruler of the Elysian Fields, home of the blessed dead.[1]

3. There had been men when King Cronus ruled but no women; Pandora, the first woman, was created on Zeus' instructions. The age of Cronus was a golden age of bliss and plenty, when the fields yielded harvests without being tilled. Since there were no women, there was no strife! Our present age, the age of Zeus, will one day come to an end, and the reign of Cronus will then be resumed. In that moment men will cease to grow older: they will grow younger. Time will repeat itself in reverse: men will be born from their graves. Women will once more cease to be necessary, and strife will disappear from the world.[2]

4. About the rituals of Cronus we know little. In Athens the most important was the festival known as Kronia. This occurred at harvest time in the first month of the year and seems to have been a sort of New Year celebration. It resembled in some ways the Roman *saturnalia* (Greek Cronus and Roman Saturn were later considered identical). Its chief feature seems to have been a ritual reversal of roles — masters waiting on slaves and so on.

What is there in all this that makes Cronus an appropriate symbol for Time? The third story certainly contains a theme about time, but how does it relate to the first two stories? Clearly the time that is involved is not time as we ordinarily tend to think of it — an endless continuum from past to future. Cronus' time is clearly an oscillation, a time that flows back

1 For detailed references see J. G. Frazer, *The Golden Bough* (3rd edn); W. H. Roscher, *Lexikon der Griechischen und Romischen Mythologie*.
2 Hasting's *Encyclopaedia of Religion and Ethics*, article 'Ages of the World' (Greek).

and forth, that is born and swallowed and vomited up, an oscillation from father to mother, mother to father and back again.

Some aspects of the story fit well enough with the views of Frazer[1] and Jane Harrison[2] about Corn Spirits and Year Spirits *(eniautos daimon)*. Cronus, as the divine reaper, cuts the 'seed' from the 'stalk' so that Mother Earth yields up her harvest. Moreover, since harvest is logically the end of a sequence of time, it is understandable enough that, given the notion of time as oscillation, the change over from year's end to year's beginning should be symbolised by a reversal of social roles; – at the end point of any kind of oscillation everything goes into reverse. Even so the interpretation in terms of vegetation magic and nature symbolism does not get us very far. Frazer and Jane Harrison count their Corn Spirits and Year Spirits by the dozen and even if Cronus does belong to the general family this does not explain why Cronus rather than any of the others should have been specifically identified as a symbol of Time personified.

My own explanation is of a more structural kind. The essence of time *(chronos)* as the Greeks conceived it, when they were not thinking simply as astronomers and geometricians, was the oscillation of vitality between two contrasted poles. The argument in Plato's *Phaedo* makes this particularly clear. Given this premise, it follows logically that the 'beginning of time' occurred at that instant when, out of an initial unity, was created not only polar opposition but also the sexual vitality that oscillates between one and the other[3] – not only God and the Virgin but the Holy Spirit as well.

Most commentators on the Cronus myth have noted simply that Cronus separates Sky from Earth,[4] but in the ideology I have been discussing the creation of time involves more than that. Not only must male be distinguished from female but one must postulate a third element, mobile and vital, which oscillates between the two. It seems clear that the Greeks thought of this third element in explicit concrete form as male semen. Rain is the semen of Zeus; fire the semen of Hephaestos; the offerings to the dead (panspermia) were baskets of seeds mixed up with phallic emblems;[5] Hermes the messenger of the gods, who takes the soul to Hades and brings back souls from the dead, is himself simply a phallus and a head and nothing more.

Given this set of metaphors Cronus' myth *does* make him 'the creator of time'. He separates sky from earth but he separates off at the same time

---

1 Frazer, *op cit.*
2 Jane Harrison, *Themis*, 1912.
3 *cf.* F. M. Cornford, 'Mystery Religions and Pre-Socratic Philosophy.' *Cambridge History Magazine*, vol. 4, 1926.
4 *e.g.* Andrew Lang, *Myth, Ritual and Religion*, 1887.
5 Harrison, *Prolegomena . . . , op cit.; Themis, op cit.*

the male vital principle which, falling to the sea reverses itself and becomes the female principle of fecundity. The shocking part of the first story, which at first seems an unnecessary gloss, contains, as one might have expected, the really crucial theme. So also in the second story the swallowing and vomiting activities of Cronus serve to create three separate categories — Zeus, the polar opposites of Zeus, and a material phallus. It is no accident that Zeus' twice born siblings are the five deities named, for each is the 'contrary' of Zeus in one of his recognized major aspects: the three females are the three aspects of womanhood, Hestia the maiden, Hera the wife, Demeter the mother; they are the opposites of Zeus in his roles as divine youth *(kouros)*, divine husband, divine father and divine son *(Dionysus)*. Hades, lord of the underworld and the dead, is the opposite of Zeus, lord of the bright day and the living; Poseidon, earth shaker, god of the sea (salt water), is the opposite of Zeus, sky shaker (thunderer), god of rain and dew.

The theme of the child which is swallowed (in whole or part) by its father and thereby given second birth, crops up in other parts of Greek mythology — *e.g.* in the case of Athena and of Dionysus. What is peculiar to the Cronus story is that it serves to establish a mythological image of interrelated contraries, a theme which recurs repeatedly in mature Greek mythology. The following comes from Cary's translation of the *Phaedo*:[1]

'We have then,' said Socrates, 'sufficiently determined this — that all things are thus produced, contraries from contraries?'

'Certainly.'

'What next? Is there also something of this kind in them, for instance, between all two contraries a mutual twofold production, from one to the other, and from the other back again . . . ?'

For men who thought in these terms, 'the beginning' would be the creation of contraries, that is to say the creation of male and female not as brother and sister but as husband and wife. My thesis then is that the philosophy of the *Phaedo* is already implicit in the gory details of the myth of Cronus. The myth is a creation myth, not a story of the beginning of the world, but a story of the beginning of time, of the beginning of becoming.

Although the climate may seem unfamiliar, this theme is not without relevance for certain topics of anthropological discussion. There is for instance Radcliffe-Brown's doctrine concerning the identification of alternating generations, whereby grandfather and grandson tend to exhibit 'solidarity' in opposition to the intervening father.[2] Or there is the stress

---

1 *Five Dialogues of Plato Bearing on Poetic Inspiration*, Everyman Edition, p. 141.
2 A. R. Radcliffe-Brown and Daryll Forde (eds), *African Systems of Kinship and Marriage*, 1950, pp. 29-31.

which Lévi-Strauss has placed upon marriage as a symbol of alliance between otherwise opposed groups.[1] Such arguments when reduced to their most abstract algebraic form may be represented by a diagram such as this:

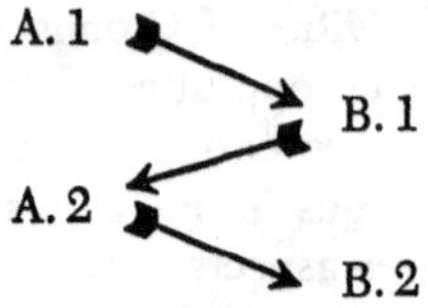

In Radcliffe-Brown's argument the As and the Bs, that are opposed yet linked, are the alternating generations of a lineage; in Lévi-Strauss', the As and the Bs are the males of contending kin groups allied by the interchange of women.

My thesis has been that the Greeks tended to conceptualize the time process as a zig-zag of this same type. They associated Cronus with the idea of time because, in a structural sense, his myth represents a separation of A from B and a creation of the initial arrow A → B, the beginning of life which is also the beginning of death.

I don't want to suggest that all primitive peoples necessarily think about time in this way, but certainly some do. The Kachins whom I mentioned earlier have a word *majan*, which, literally, ought to mean 'woman affair'. They use it in three main contexts to mean (a) warfare, (b) a love-song, and (c) the weft threads of a loom. This seems to us an odd concatenation yet I fancy the Greeks would have understood it very well. Penelope sits at her loom, the shuttle goes back and forth, back and forth, love and war, love and war;[2] and what does she weave? You can guess without looking up your *Odyssey* —, a *shroud* of course, the time of Everyman. 'Tis love that makes the world go round; but women are the root of all evil.

E. R. Leach

[1] C. Lévi-Strauss, 'L'analyse structurale en linguistique et en anthropologie.' *Word*, August, 1945.

[2] For the specific Greek associations of weaving and time and the story of Penelope, see references to *kairos* in Onians, *op cit*. Likewise Ares, god of war, is paramour of Aphrodite, goddess of love.

COMMUNICATION BY MEANS OF GONGS AND OTHER INSTRUMENTS IN CENTRAL AFRICA

Human speech as a means of communication involves the interplay of several factors, among which we can distinguish: (a) phonetic elements, involving the quality of the sounds emitted by the voice; (b) tonetic elements, involving the pitch of the sounds emitted by the voice; (c) syllable prominence, involving variations in amplitude of the sounds emitted and changes in the rhythm of consecutive elements of speech; and (d) gesture. For a proper understanding of the way in which wooden gongs and other instruments can serve as a means of representing and transmitting language elements, it is necessary to study in further detail the second, and to a less extent the third, of these factors.

Tonal variations play a part in all human speech, except perhaps in whispered communications, where factor (a) is of greater importance. In most languages, tone is significant for differentiating interrogatory elements and for imparting emotional colour to the spoken words. It also serves to give coherence to separate groups of language elements, a falling series of tones indicating in many languages the end of a period. In some language groups, notably those found in Central Africa, however, tonal elements, in addition to determining interrogative forms and giving emotional colour and coherence to speech, play an important part in lexical and grammatical differentiation. Thus in Lokele,[1] the

[1] J. F. Carrington, 'The Tonal Structure of Kele (Lokele).' *African Studies*, Johannesburg, 1943.

language of a Bantu-speaking people living in the Stanleyville area of the Belgian Congo, the vocables represented as ítiluwé (I didn't fish) and ítilúwé (I don't know)[1] are distinguishable only because of the tonetic alternance in the third syllable. Similarly, the two grammatically distinct vocables: áyéke (do not let him come) and áyeke (let him come) are only distinguishable because of the tonetic alternance: yé/ye of the second syllable. Very many examples of such lexical and grammatical tonal differences could be adduced from Lokele and many other languages of the Central Congo and other linguistic zones in Africa.

It should be noted that the actual pitch given to a syllable by the speaker is not recorded here. This 'speech tone' is the resultant of the action of the essential tones or 'tonemes' recorded and tonal variations imposed upon the essential tones according to the emotional colour given to his language by the speaker, to the position of the linguistic elements in the group as a whole, to the form—interrogatory, declamatory or otherwise—being used, and so on. Whatever the actual pitch adopted for the syllables of: áyeke (let him come), for instance, the speaker must always be careful to make a drop in pitch from the first to the second syllable. The actual differences in frequencies between the two sounds emitted is unimportant for grammatical distinction provided it is sufficient to be noticeable as a drop in pitch to the hearer.

It will be noted that only two essential tones are here distinguished, though the number of 'speech tones' will be very numerous. Lokele and all the neighbouring 'tone languages' are alike in having only two essential tones. In some African languages, however, more than two essential tones are found. Three such tones are recorded for Ibo (Nigeria) and for some Sudanic languages in the north-east corner of Belgian Congo (e.g., Gbaka). Where linguistic writers speak of more numerous tones, it is often found that the term 'tone' as used by them does not correspond with what we have here described as 'essential tone'. Some authors would further distinguish as a separate 'tone' the rising-tone or falling-tone heard in such Lokele words as: bɔ̌mwi (five) and asŏtâ (she has born). Study of the language shows however that these elements are better represented as: bɔɔ́mwi and asóoótá, so that the rising and falling tones are resolved into consecutive high and low tones on similar phonetic elements. A falling tone may also be due to the position of an essentially high tone at the end of a vocable so that its essentially high tone is masked by the action of 'sentence-tone'.

Syllable prominence may also be significant for grammatical and lexical differentiation of language elements. The distinction between the two Lingala[2] vocables: nakokanisa (I shall think) and nákokanisa (let me

[1] High tones are marked with an acute accent; low tones remain unmarked.

[2] Lingala is the 'lingua franca' of the riverine area of Central Congo. There is no gong-language associated with it, but it is a typical bitonemal language like Lokele. See M. Guthrie, *Grammaire et Dictionnaire Lingala*. Cambridge, 1939.

make equal to . . .) is partly brought about by the tonetic alternance na/ná on the first syllable, but is also considerably helped by the difference in syllable prominence of the following syllables. Prominent syllables are underlined in these two examples; in the spoken word such prominence is achieved by greater amplitude of the emitted sound and by a lengthening of the syllable to be stressed. The main stress is here found on the initial syllable of the root while a secondary stress develops on the penultimate syllable when this is some distance from the initial syllable of the root.

When linguistic elements of a language such as Lokele are used as a basis for broadcast messages on a wooden talking-gong, the speech factors represented on the instrument are, firstly the essential tones of the linguistic elements and secondly, the rhythm of the syllables of these elements. Phonetic factors are never reproduced. Tonal variations associated with emotional colour and sentence position are not reproduced as such, but their significance is rendered by conventional methods which will be mentioned below.

THE GONGS USED FOR BROADCASTING

The signalling gong of the Lokele tribe is a wooden log varying in size from about 60 centimetres to 3 centimetres in length and from 30 centimetres to 120 centimetres in diameter. A special wood is almost always used (*Pterocarpus Soyauxii*) which also gives the red powder used to smear on the body for ornamentation during the dance. Drum-making and gong-making with this wood are especially associated with one village in the central area occupied by the Lokele. The cylindrical log of red heart-wood is hollowed out through a narrow slit-like mouth by means of an adze, curved axe-blades and chisels. The gong-maker is careful to hollow out the log more under one lip of the mouth than under the other. The former emits a lower note (called the 'voice of the male') when the lip is beaten with the rubber-covered sticks used in signalling, while the lip over the less hollowed side of the instrument emits a relatively higher pitched note (called the 'voice of the female'). Many gong carvers leave a ridge of wood between the two differentially hollowed halves of the instrument; they call this ridge 'the backbone' of the gong.

The relative pitch of the two notes emitted by a gong varies from one instrument to another. Many gong-makers approximate to an interval of a musical major third, but intervals varying from one musical tone to an octave can be heard. The actual frequencies of each lip vary also from instrument to instrument. This is of no importance for adequate message transmission, but it can be of great help in picking out the beats of a particular gong (and so understanding what the beater of that instrument is 'saying') when several gongs are being used in one area. This rarely occurs, however; politeness rules that one gong has precedence over others in a restricted area such as a single village or village section.

A two-toned gong is adequate to broadcast messages in a language like Lokele which has two distinct essential tones. The instrument simply reproduces on the 'female' lip all the syllables having high essential tones in the linguistic elements forming the basis of the communication, while the 'male' lip similarly reproduces the tones of syllables having a low essential tone in these linguistic elements. The gong indeed broadcasts tonal melodies; these are however not quite the same as the tonal melodies of the spoken language because only essential tones are reproduced on the two lips of the wooden gong. Emotional and positional tonal elements which raise or lower the essential tones in actual speech cannot be reproduced as such on the gong with its two fixed notes. Thus, all the members of the following two sample series of Lokele vocables will be represented in the same way by the gong because their tonal patterns are identical:

three low tones, represented by three beats on the male lip:	one low tone followed by two high tones, represented by one beat on the male lip plus two beats on the female lip:
lomata (manioc)	balíá (water)
likɔndɔ (plantain)	baítá (oil)
bɔkɔkɔ (log of wood; gong)	bokálí (wife)[1]
boseka (girl)	yeétó (metal)
lokela (poison)	

It is clear that if the gong broadcasts used simply the vocables given above, a hearer could not possibly understand whether the message were calling for manioc, for wooden logs, for plantain or for poison, when three low notes should be heard. Nor could he distinguish among the many meanings for the tonal pattern: low-high-low. The broadcast language does become intelligible to the hearer, however, because the objects listed above are represented, not by the single vocables used for speech (where phonetic elements give the significance that the tonal melody cannot give alone), but by a whole group of linguistic elements, often of a proverb-like nature, the complete tonal melody of which is quite characteristic. For the first of the series given above, we must broadcast as follows:

manioc:	lomata otíkala kóndo	(the manioc remains in the fallow land)
plantain:	likɔndɔ líbotúmbela	(the plantain which must be propped up when the fruit is ripe)

[1] The corresponding vocable in the spoken language is: wálí. The gong-language may be here perpetuating an older form of this vocable.

log:	bɔkɔkɔ wá olondó	(log of olondo-wood)
girl:	boseka âtilakɛndɛ́ liŋginda	(a girl doesn't travel about in the company of other girls)
poison:	loleka lótí lesaelo	(the poison whose virulence never abates)

And for the second series:

water:	balíá balɔkɔila	(water of the 'lɔkɔila'-vine)
oil:	baítá olóŋgó lalitoko líbotukola	(oil, child of the palmtree)
wife:	bokálí labalaŋga	(the woman with (?) yams)
metal:	yeétó yálikoŋgá	(metal of spears)

None of the tonal patterns of these short linguistic groups is the same as another. Thus the addition of further linguistic elements to vocables which have the same essential tone melody serves completely to characterize these vocables. Gong-beaters must learn the conventional groups of words associated with each object referred to in broadcast messages and must learn to recall the phonetic elements of these groups when they hear the essential tonal melodies on a neighbouring gong.

Actions of common occurrence in village life as well as objects have their characteristic phrases of which the essential tones alone are reproduced on the gong-lips:

spoken:		beaten:
asóoinwá	(he returns)	asóoinólá batíndí la mbísa asóoinólá bakolo mbísa (he has returned his feet, he has returned his legs)
asóowá	(he is dead)	asóosílélá bolímó wá akalékalé kondábaúki kondânyɛlɛ (he has given up the spirit, stretched out on his back on the clods, on the ground)
tóleke	(let's eat)	tőkɛsɛ bilémá yá loúsá kondâlikɔkɔ lyá kíŋgó (let us put the things of outside into the knot of the throat)

The gong-beater's task is further complicated by the fact that similar proverb-like phrases are used to represent all the male members of the tribe; villages and village sections have also their characteristic gong-names. The gong-name of Batoko, a young man from the Foma village of Yaotike, about 70 kilometres west of Stanleyville is as follows:

(a) botó kweékweé bakolo bálɔkɛndɔ	As the head nods, the legs journey forward;

	bɔtɔ́ndɔ bótókikólá njásɔ	the important man arranges palavers to suit himself;
(b)	wána wabolemba bótílaótókó laoto	child of the bad spirit with no kinsmen;
(c)	bokáná wábélakweísáká bolemba	mother's village: Yaotike (they overcome evil spirits)

24 There are three parts to this complete gong-name: (a) is the name given to Batoko by his father as soon as he was able to understand the gong-language and use it; (b) is the gong-name of his father; and (c) is the name of his mother's village. (The fact that Batoko's father and mother are both from Yaotike is composed of several distinct and inter-marrying sections.) Examples of the names of other villages in the area:

Yatuka	bááká baŋgénɛ́ liandé	(they were masters of the river)
Yaowamya	bááká lalítílatwé nɔŋgɔ́	(they could not be defeated by attacks at dawn)
Yakoso	afaká kolaalɛ́mbu	(? of doubtful meaning; possibly the names of two ancestors)

Rhythmic changes as well as tonal melodies play a part in making the characteristic, conventional phrases of the gong-messages intelligible to hearers. Gong-beaters make no attempt to reproduce the syllable prominence of speech by varying the amplitude of the gong-sounds, but they do follow closely the rhythmic sequence of the syllables being broadcast. In rare cases rhythm may be significant for meaning, such as in the Lokele gong-language elements:

botandalakɔkɔ	canoe (literally: log to walk upon)
tolakondeloko	we shall have people grow up among us (part of a phrase to indicate astonishment)

Here the tonal melodies are identical, but rhythm changes and makes the gong-sounds representing these two elements quite distinct.

We have already stated that emotional tones of speech are not reproduced on the gong. Conventional phrases, however, broadcast in the same way as any other gong-language elements, serve to indicate sorrow, exhortation, astonishment, anger and to enforce commands. For instance, when an incident occurs which produces surprise, the gong-message may begin with:

tolakondeloko tolaóteloko	literally: we shall have people grow up among us; we shall have children born to us. The suggestion here is that of: 'but this sort of thing we shall not see'. Compare: 'I never seen the like since I was born!'

Death messages are always prefaced by an exhortation to cry:

wálelaka wálelaka wálelaka	you will cry, you will cry,
bilelí kondá baíso	tears in the eyes;
bolelo kondáɔnɔkɔ	wailing in the mouth.

Anger at an insulting message on the gong from an enemy would be expressed by the injured party on his own instrument in the following way:

kpɛí kpɛí kpɛí kpɛí	ho! ho! ho!
kokɛsɛ́ liói libé libé	sending an evil, evil word
likolo kondáúsé	up into the air?

The linguistic element: kpɛí is an onomatopoeic rendering of the sound produced by beating the two lips of the gong simultaneously. This device is frequently used by gong-beaters to punctuate their messages. It corresponds indeed to an indented line in written communications. The full stop of written language is indicated by a pause between successive sections of the gong-message. Special signals are used for opening and closing the communication. Such are, for instance:

íto' íto íto íto	look out!	(Lokele)
túkútúkútúkútúkútúkútúkútúkú túkútúkú		
dɔkɔdɔkɔdɔkɔdɔkɔdɔkɔdɔkɔdɔkɔdɔkɔdɔkɔ		(Mba)

where the linguistic elements simply represent onomatopoeically the sounds of the gong. Lokele gong-beaters often finish their message with: líko ndé liói lyáɔnɔkɔ . . . such is the word of the mouth of . . . and proceed to add the name of the person responsible for the message.

OTHER INSTRUMENTS USED

Since the basis of gong broadcasting in Central Africa is the possibility of representing the two essential tones of linguistic elements and their rhythmic patterns by means of two differently pitched sounds of a wooden gong, it is clear that any method of producing two distinct tones would serve to send messages of this type. In point of fact, many such methods are used in conjunction with or in the absence of gongs. Skin-topped drums can be used, for instance. Among the Ashanti of West Africa,[1] messages are broadcast on two drums one of which has a low note and is referred to as the male drum, while the other, smaller and having a higher note, is described as the female drum. A single skin-topped drum can be used, but in this case the membrane must be stopped by the hand or the leg in order to produce a higher note to reproduce the high essential tone of the linguistic elements to be broadcast. Two-toned horns are common in many parts of Africa. These are often side-blown horns, the thumb opening or closing a hole at the tip

[1] R. S. Rattray, 'The Drum-language of West Africa.' *Journal of the African Society*, 1922-23.

of the horn in order to give a high or low note and so represent the two essential tones of the language used. Whistles are commonly used in the same way.[1] Sometimes a third note is reported for these whistles, but it is found to be used to punctuate the message only and not to represent a third essential tone. (The writer has shown this to be true for some wooden gongs from Congo where three notes were regarded as representing three tones of the language broadcast; the third tone is, however, used only for punctuation.)[2]

A stringed instrument is used among the Olombo tribe (neighbours of the Lokele in the Stanleyville area) to broadcast messages to a small group of people during a game of 'hide-and-seek', played to mystify strangers who do not understand the linguistic basis of the messages. The writer has also heard a simple wooden pole with an oval section (actually the broken stem of a canoe paddle) used to indicate to youths undergoing initiation rites, the initial measures of a dance accompanied by singing. Struck across the greater diameter of the oval section, the pole emitted a high note while, when struck across the smaller diameter, it gave a low tone. The leader of the youths beat out in this way the tonal melody of part of the song to which they were to dance; immediately the initiates were expected to take up the song indicated and begin to dance to it. Those not able to do so were hit over the head with the heavy stick used to beat the resounding pole.

Whistling by means of the lips is frequently used to send messages over a small distance; it is often associated with magical practices. The human voice can be used too, shouts of two different pitches being broadcast to imitate the essential tones of the linguistic elements of the message. Such shouted messages are efficacious in the forest and on the river over distances where phonetic elements could not be heard but where the alternance of two differently pitched sounds is clearly audible. Lokele fishermen shout kɛ or lɛ for the low-pitched essential tone and kí or lí for the high tone. The use of lɛ rather than kɛ and lí rather than kí depends on the rhythm of the consecutive elements of the message. Thus, the two elements already noted as being distinguishable by rhythm alone, would be shouted as:

tolakondeloko kɛ lɛ kɛ lɛ kɛ kɛ
botandalakɔkɔ kɛ kɛ kɛ lɛ kɛ kɛ

GONG LANGUAGE AND SPOKEN LANGUAGE

We have stated that the gong reproduces the essential tones and the rhythmic patterns of language elements. We must consider now the relation between the linguistic elements forming the basis of gong mes-

[1] L. Labouret, 'Langage tambourine et sifflé.' *Bull. du Comite d'Etudes Hist. et Scient. de l'A.E.F.*, no. 1, 1923; G. Hulstaert, 'Notes sur les instruments de musique à l'Equateur.' *Congo*, 1935, and 'De telefoon der Nkundo.' *Anthropos*, 1935.
[2] J. F. Carrington, *A Comparative Study of Some Central African Gong Languages.* Brussels, 1949.

sages and the spoken language of the tribes using gongs and other instruments.

The greater part of the gong-language used by the Lokele people corresponds exactly with the spoken language. This correspondence is so close that the gong gives a valuable means of checking and learning tonal patterns of spoken Lokele. A similar use of the gong has been advocated for other Central African languages such as Luba. Linguistic elements occur in the gong-language, however, which are not used in the spoken language. These can often be shown to be archaic forms of the spoken language, preserved in the stereotyped conventional phrases handed down by one generation of gong-beaters to the next. There are also elements whose meaning is doubtful, gong-beaters giving them phonetic values but being unable to supply equivalents in the spoken language. These forms may be phonetically very diverse when several gong-beaters are consulted, but the tonal patterns are always identical. Thus in the two contiguous villages of Bandio and Yalɛmba (Basoko district of Belgian Congo) the gong-name of the European is given variously as: botutu bólimbambalimba and botiti bóliŋgoŋgoliŋgo.

Many tribes, however, seem to have adopted the gong-broadcasting from neighbours and do not use their own language for sending messages on musical instruments. The Ena (Wagenya) of the Stanley Falls use Lokele as a linguistic basis for their gong messages and can themselves understand the gong messages of the Lokele villages. Their spoken language is quite different from that of the Lokele. The Mba tribe has, on the other hand, appropriated linguistic elements from a number of neighbouring groups, in order to constitute a thesaurus of gong-language elements for their own use. We can distinguish elements of Lokele, Olombo and Aŋba gong-languages as well as those based on spoken Mba. In the Basoko area of Belgian Congo, the language of a relatively small group of people—the Sɔ tribe—has become the gong-language of the villages speaking as many as ten different languages.

SOME POINTS FOR FURTHER RESEARCH

It will have been clear that the linguistic elements of the gong-messages used by Central African and other peoples are an important form of oral literature. Their study can elucidate many points of difficulty in current historical, linguistic and ethnographical investigation as well as being valuable for their literary content as such. Unfortunately, the present-day generation of Congo youth shows little or no interest in the gong-messages, and knowledge of the language is rapidly dying out. Records of as many as possible of these gong-languages should be gathered in permanent form while gifted gong-beaters are still available.

The methods of broadcasting in areas where languages are undoubtedly tri-tonemal ought to be studied. It has been suggested that two gongs, giving four distinct notes, may be used adequately to broadcast these linguistic elements. On the other hand, the use of two gongs is common to certain 'ritual' broadcasting in the Stanleyville area where the linguistic elements have only two tones. The gong-beater broadcasts his main message on a high-pitched gong and punctuates this with repetitions of a conventional phrase on the low-pitched instrument.

28 Further investigation is necessary into methods of message transmission where single skin-topped drums are used, as in East Africa.[1] Linguistic elements are given as a basis for such messages in some cases, but if only one tone is used the method of representing essential elements of language cannot be the same as that we have described for the Lokele and other Central African tribes. Two-toned gongs are reported from other continents as being used for message transmission, e.g., among the Jibaros of Peru and Eastern Ecuador[2] and from numerous stations in Melanesia and Polynesia.[3] It will be of considerable interest to know the relationship between signals transmitted and linguistic bases often given for these. Again, some records state that, though the instruments have two tones, only one is used for broadcasting. In this case, the method of transmission of the message cannot be the same as that described for the Congo.

John F. Carrington

---

[1] J. Roscoe, *The Bakitara.* Cambridge, 1923.
[2] P. Rivet, 'Les Indiens Jibaros.' *l'Anthropologie*, 1908.
[3] F. Speiser, *Ethnographische Materialen aus dem Neuene Hebriden und den Banks-Inseln.* Berlin, 1923; and D. H. Meijer, 'Das Alarmsystem der Javanischen Dorfpolizei.' *Archiv für Anthropologie*, Bd. 23, 1935.

VEBLEN'S SYSTEM OF SOCIAL SCIENCE[1]

Veblen was a man who all his life was abnormally sensitive to constraint. At the various universities where he was a bird of passage, as an early-vintage Bohemian, he had few ties to colleagues and hardly any to students. He avoided commitment to the various radical movements that sought to embrace him. And his irony, too, was a way of avoiding entangling alliances with people and causes, or with the reader. He was at his best in uncovering the hidden assumptions of other economists, other epochs, or other social classes, while he avoided uncovering his own assumptions, rather naively believing that he was a matter-of-fact 'opaque' scientist unhurriedly pursuing the truth. He proffered his own, often subtle insights as everyday notions, pretending that the common man had known these things all along, and that only the academician, with the trained incapacity of his craft, could possibly fail to see them. Typically, he introduced some reforming plan of his own with the words 'it has been suggested', as if it were somebody else's idea; of his projected Soviet of Technicians he stated that it 'will apparently' take such and such a form, as if he were describing some highly probable event; or he would refer to some hope of his as the direction in which the brute trend and drift of things are tending.

---

1 I have drawn heavily, for this article, on my forthcoming book, *Thorstein Veblen: A Critical Interpretation*, to be published by Charles Scribner's Sons in their Twentieth Century Library. I am indebted for many helpful suggestions to Staughton Lynd.

He not only submitted himself to a thorough-going canon of impersonality but urged his readers, too, to submit to the inevitable, to the ongoing technological forces that would sweep the rest of culture in their train. Fearing constraint, he sought a discipline — economics — that he wanted to make as rigorous as possible, and that he interpreted as a cold Darwinian science of the evolutionary drift of the industrial arts (and of the pecuniary machinations which temporarily blocked their advance). The personal motives leading him to such selectivity must have been powerful ones — not unrelated, I suspect, to his admiration for a cold, domineering, and technically minded father — but the intellectual influences upon him — Sumner, Darwin, Spencer, and others — were also powerful; it was an age in which men, seeking to subdue their own unruly passions, also sought to order the universe, to build majestic, one might almost say, patriarchal, systems.

Compared to these other system-builders, Veblen was too 'passive' to force his data into a tight theoretical scheme, but he nevertheless wrote with sly aggression against the data. In the chapter on 'The Higher Learning' in *The Theory of the Leisure Class* there is the revealing comment that it would not be difficult but would be mechanically tedious to trace the correlation between growth of collegiate wealth in midwest colleges and 'the date of acceptance — first into acceptance and then into imperative vogue — of evening dress for men and of the decollete for women, as the scholarly vestments proper to occasions of learned solemnity or to the seasons of social amenity within the college circle.' Generalization here appears as a form of labour-saving machinery. There is no necessary harm in that — Veblen is the opposite extreme from the stereotype of sociologist who, with no philosophical training, consumes his time affixing exact degrees of significance to insignificant correlations and never gets around to discovering anything new about society. But the danger lies in the possibility that Veblen shut himself off from much that was new by his very propensity for abstraction and generalization. Had he in this case, for instance, made an actual investigation, he might have discovered that, if wealth were great enough, it might induce indifference to dress, or that there were denominational differences irrespective of wealth, or rural-urban ones, and so on — all the buzzing, blooming confusion of American life which Veblen somehow, thinking he understood it, did not continue to grapple with.

THE QUEST FOR CERTAINTY

The search for theoretical consistency seems to us today to be truncated, to stop too soon, to have too great a fear of ambiguity and bewilderment in the face of the universe. It is not so much that Veblen jumps to conclusions: he starts with the conviction that conclusions there must be. Thus, whereas he greatly admired Hume's scepticism, on the whole he applied it as a debunker of capitalism rather than as a radical self-critique. And as his life wore on, he seems to have become steadily less open to new evidence, or even interested in any that did not sustain previously cherished views. The result is that, though his output spans a period of nearly forty years, one finds little unfolding, little development in it — only a change towards greater rigidity. When he first comes on the scene he is already a mature thinker: as an undergraduate at Carleton, he was debunking theology, satirically commenting on his fellow-students (as he had earlier fastened nicknames on the Veblens' neighbors), and following with interest the literary and political iconoclasts of the day, such as Ibsen and Henry George. To this kind of literary iconoclasm, Veblen later added the iconoclastic tendencies in post-Darwinian science; thus armoured, he sought to direct economics away from its abstractions towards 'the practical exigencies of modern industrial life' (*The Place of Science in Modern Civilisation*, p. 81). Yet, since men cannot live and work without abstractions, Veblen's picture of 'modern industrial life' (the phrase is itself an abstraction) is strewn with undigested lumps of the now largely discredited psychologies and anthropologies of the late 19th century. And since, as I have suggested, Veblen could not long tolerate uncertainty he sought escape from the ambiguities of his cross-disciplinary efforts by building new webs of abstraction, such as his instinct theory or his theory of evolutionary stages through which men had passed from Savagery to Barbarism (of several sorts) to Capitalism — with Socialism at the far end. Indeed, Veblen's partial failure helps us to see how much more difficult it is than he had supposed to harmonize the abstractions of economics with those of anthropology and psychology; this is an intellectual task still far from accomplished, but one which we can now see is not facilitated by substituting one set of fashionable abstractions called 'reality' for another.[1] A greater willingness to accept confusion and temporary inconsistencies in theoretical framework might have enabled Veblen to develop rather than restate his views, and to perceive a few more of the then-unadvertised events that were to transform the everyday life of man in his own life-time, such as the beginnings of assembly-line production, and the first stirrings of colonial revolt.

To be sure, there are times when Veblen appears to recognize the limits beyond which his thought could not go. He now and again declares that the impersonal Darwinian forces that move mankind are obscure and, in their cumulative working out, unpredictable; occasionally, he will speak

---

1 It should be evident that I am not contending that a fear of constraint combined with a quest for certainty is uniquely Veblenian: such attitudes are of course widespread in the academic culture, though some fields are more appealing than others to men of this type (sociology perhaps more than psychology, for example, and economics more in Veblen's day than now, when it has become immensely larger, more successful, more organized).

of the evidence he has marshalled as 'not unquestionably convincing' (see, e.g., *Theory of the Leisure Class*, p. 361). But usually this kind of disclaimer turns out to be a preface to prophecy – and prophecy based always on the assumption that there is such a thing as a social *system*, that society is systematic and not chaotic, that men are not, like kings with their court jesters, able to make fools of their scientists' accounts of them.

It is not surprising that the world today, despite all Veblen's effort to catch 'the main drift', is not the one he foretold. And yet he did produce a number of startling predictions. Not so much his forcible systematizations as the detachment he achieved, or, more likely, possessed from the beginning and accepted, seems to have been one essential element in his anticipation of the aggressive potentialities of an industrialized Japanese feudalism; of the change in the Second International toward patriotism in World War I; of the Great Depression; and, if he did not predict World War II in so many words, at least he had a belief at the time of Versailles that another war was coming, and had an awareness of the military power that revived German feudal attitudes would have.

Explaining to the British in the summer of 1952 what she regards as the increasing conservatism of American academic life, Mary McCarthy stated that professors who take consultant jobs in business and government get to understand too much to be able to criticize – but in a curious way this close connection also limits understanding, for it is hard not to share the hopes and fears of those who treat us well. Veblen did not suffer the loss such luck can bring – at least until it was too late for him to change. The pessimism induced by his personal tragedy prepared him to foresee the disappointments of the hopes of liberals and socialists alike. The scepticism he looked for in the engineer and the skilled industrial worker[1] was in reality a projection of his own multiple alienation, as immigrant's son, farmer's son, unsuccessful husband, and itinerant, barely tolerated scholar; but it was this alienation which put him far enough from our society to view it, for long suspended stretches, as a curious mechanism.

THE INSTINCT OF WORKMANSHIP

If there is a basic entity in Veblen's system, it is the 'instinct of workmanship': an assumed human propensity for activity tailored to the efficient achievement of a goal. The instinct represented for Veblen the constructive element in human life. It is the only one not largely immersed in the destructive element – emulation, business chicane, imperialism, the

[1] So far as I know, Veblen never personally discovered any workers in large urban industry who fitted the picture he held of them. But he did discover the Wobblies, the I.W.W., who were mainly the least urbanized and industrialized workers — they were casual farm labourers, lumbermen, Western miners, etc. It was among these men that Veblen in fact found the saucy irreverence and political intransigeance he admired.

corruption of universities by businessmen, and so on – or professionally preoccupied with demolishing the assumptions of other economists.

In the opening pages of *The Instinct of Workmanship and the State of the Industrial Arts*, the instinct of workmanship is sketched out as a tendency towards craftsmanship as an end in itself, and towards the accomplishment of constructive work – that is, by its very nature, it guides both ends and means, and may lead to confusion between them. As a tendency towards craftsmanship for its own sake, the instinct of workmanship may be thought of (though Veblen himself never put it quite this way) as a manual equivalent to a second Veblenian instinct, that of 'idle curiosity', as he termed a playful surplusage of interest in the world, beyond pragmatic requirements. And in its other aspect, as a concern for useful workmanship in the interest of the species, the instinct of workmanship may be linked with still another Veblenian instinct, the 'parental bent', a kind of generalized solicitude not only for one's own young but for the future of mankind.

These very linkages show that the instinct of workmanship, in Veblen's usage, is not oriented to specific goals but is diffuse, as much an assistance to other instincts in effectively reaching their ends as a definite drive. The instinct thus enters into all human activity in Veblen's view, even into activity running counter to its ulterior end of species-advancing construction. Thus, had Veblen lived long enough to read Stephen Potter's satiric books on 'Gamesmanship' and 'Lifemanship', he might have observed how the manœuvers of Potter's heroes deploy the highest arts of workmanship in precisely the sportsmanlike, invidious, and emulative manner Veblen most despised; indeed, he was already inclined to think that the British gentleman was the planet's noblest flowering of effortful, workmanlike futility. But the instinct of workmanship, though periodically defeated by its own zeal, is not wholly at the mercy of whatever conventional pragmatic, and foolish ends a society may hold dear; it serves at once to accomplish and to alter those ends, for it is an active force – something like 'intelligence' in John Dewey's system, or the 'strain to consistency' in Sumner's – tending to bend men's activity away from mere habitual and mindless activity towards the (as Veblen saw it) natural ends of production and of concern for the young.

By calling workmanship an instinct, however, Veblen emphasized conscious human purposes less than biological drives, and cultivated purposes less than natural or inherited ones. And by stressing the ways in which custom could channel workmanship into the use of self-defeating means, he was choosing the more pessimistic Social Darwinism of Sumner as against the more optimistic Social Darwinism of Spencer or Lester Ward.

More often than not, Veblen appears in the role of a debunker of exhortations to men's reason or of historical predictions, such as Marxism (which he could not deride enough for its 'pre-Darwinian' elements), which rest on the predictor's notion of what it would be rational for men in a given situation to do.

Yet, taking his work as a whole, we see that Veblen was less inclined to stress the irrational in man than were many others who sought to ground a systematic social science in biology or physiology – Freud, for instance.[1]

The very fact that he uses 'instinct' loosely and often metaphorically – students of Veblen in fact differ as to how many instincts he postulated – saves him from the common 19th century notion that society is biology writ large. Moreover, since his instincts as we shall see have a bent to succor man rather than destroy him, since they work together rather than pull apart, they seem almost to possess a kind of situational 'intelligence'.

Veblen faced analogous problems in deciding between an emphasis on the wholeness of human behaviour and an emphasis on compartmentalization. He differed from apperceptionist psychology in insisting on the purposeful *activity* of human beings, and the same line of thought led him to underline the *Gestalt* in behaviour. In *The Instinct of Workmanship*, he declared (p. 40):

> In all their working, the human instincts are . . . incessantly subject to mutual 'contamination' whereby the working of any one is incidentally affected by the bias and proclivities in all the rest.

This must be so because the human organism is of one piece, and what it does in one department of life under the dominant ægis of one instinct, will affect its behaviour in all other departments. Further, the instincts themselves are not separate biologically. Veblen asserted (*ibid.*, p. 11):

> . . . the common run of human instincts are not to be conceived as severally discrete and elementary proclivities. The same physiological processes enter in some measure, though in varying proportions, into the functioning of each. In instinctive action, the individual acts as a whole, and in the conduct which emerges under the driving force of these instinctive dispositions the part which each several instinct plays is a matter of more or less, not of exclusive direction.

But as he grew older and more bitter, Veblen's emphasis on the rationality and wholeness of human behaviour grew less and less. Symbolic and

---

1 Ernest Jones' forthcoming life of Freud describes in detail the influence upon him of Brücke, Helmholtz, and other scientific pioneers — and of his achievement of a partial emancipation from their methodology. In my article, 'Authority and Liberty in the Structure of Freud's Thought', *Psychiatry*, 8:167-187, 1950, I try to indicate the democratizing motives implicit in this sort of reductionism — a theme one can trace also in Veblen.

partly productive of this change was the increasing influence upon him of Jacques Loeb, a brilliant biologist, who accepted the instinctual approach, but retained the associationist view that consciousness was an epiphenomenon and need not be involved in scientific study of psychology. His views are evident, for example, in Veblen's description of revolution in *Absentee Ownership* by the title of one of Loeb's books, *Forced Movements, Tropisms, and Animal Conduct.* 35

THE REASON OF CURIOSITY

As already implied, reason sometimes appeared in the wavering purposefulness of workmanship in Veblen's scheme, but was more fully embodied in his instinct of idle curiosity. Indeed, it was in an Enlightenment spirit of aristocratic curiosity that Veblen dissociated himself from pragmatism, which he regarded as the common-sensical manipulation of conventions for utilitarian ends. Yet this dissociation was at best partial and intermittent. For instance, between the chapter on the higher learning in *The Theory of the Leisure Class* (1899) and the book by that name (1918), Veblen's attitude towards the institutionalization of curiosity in scholarship as over against vocational training seems to have changed decidedly. In the former book he is on the side of vocational training, treating scholarship only as a furbelow to the gentlemanly life and a hazard for truly useful work; thus, he says that the quasi-theological and foggy trappings of academic ritual originated in the university and spread from there to the lower and vocational schools (pp. 369-370 in the Modern Library edition). In *The Higher Learning,* however, he insists on the segregation of the pure research of the university from the contaminating practical bent of the vocational school. He now contrasts the instinct of idle curiosity with *both* workmanship (or industry) and predation (or business) — usually making a very clear dichotomy between workmanship and predation. In *The Higher Learning,* that is, both workmanlike and predatory activities are lumped together and condemned as unduly practical: Veblen seemed to want to protect the universities against the 'vulgar' modern mechanism for which he was ordinarily the spokesman. But the very concept of idle curiosity, which forbids a functional role to the instinct, prevented Veblen from rationalizing the higher learning as part of a defensible division of labour between instincts or between institutions. Failing to develop a theory of play, curiosity, and other 'surplus' motives and activities, he was forced back on a traditional conception of the life of reason as a thing in itself, divorced from action, art, and feeling.

ENTER EMULATION

These three instincts — workmanship, idle curiosity, and care for the young (parental bent) — are for Veblen, then, not only a substratum of human nature but a source of moral absolutes. By means of these instincts Veblen goes to some pains to preserve the distinction between ends and means: these three activities are or can be ends in themselves, while all other lines of action are pragmatic, directed toward some ulterior end. Beyond that, what the three Veblenian instincts have in common is a turning outward from the individual to nature or society, a merging of the individual through work, observation, or solicitude in the processes surrounding him. The instinct of the idle curiosity and the instinct of workmanship (in its aspect of pure craftsmanship) involve what Veblen calls a 'non-reverent sense of æsthetic congruity with the environment' (*Theory of the Leisure Class*, p. 333), or again 'the sense of communion with the environment, or with the generic life process' (*ibid.*, p. 334). Workmanship for the sake of serviceability, and the parental bent, merge into this sense also, though with the emphasis on the human environment and the human life process.

Veblen's decision to regard as most fundamental these three instincts, sharing one common quality — at a time when many psychologists were positing a dozen or more instincts — was not only a concealed moral choice. It was also the product of his immersion in the evolutionary methodology of Darwinism. A fundamental tenet of this methodology was that the environment exercises a most rigorous selective pressure upon the organisms within it, and that only organisms perfectly adapted to the environment can survive. Now if man's genetic make-up was fixed in his prehistory, when his competitive struggle was presumably at its grimmest — and Veblen believed this was the case — then human nature could have afforded, so to speak, only those constituents most conducive to the survival of the species. The instinct of workmanship was therefore a brute biological necessity: 'as a matter of selective necessity, man is an agent' (*ibid.*, p. 15). Man could not have survived had he possessed compelling needs catering to his individual welfare at the expense of the species: such needs were luxuries which could develop only as, in the course of history, men create wealth enough to make them secure in their environment. But Veblen did not regard these late-coming attitudes, such as pugnacity, as 'really' instincts — though once in a while he loosely uses the term — he rules them out with the Pavlovian argument that man had not been conditioned to their exercise for a long enough time: only the primordial trinity were 'natural'. In his essay on 'Christian Morals and the Competitive System', Veblen argued that the Christian attitudes of serviceability and brotherhood would survive the late-coming attitudes of competition and emulation because closer to man's instinctive base, and because they are older and more thorough-going in terms of historical habituation.

But there was still another reason Veblen had for thinking workmanship would win out over the late-comer, wastemanship, namely his Puritanical and ascetic feeling that the surplus men could produce would never be great enough to permit them to survive in the face of wasteful, futile, and destructive conduct. As Darwin took over Malthus' perspective of a bitter race between man and his means of subsistence — leading Darwin to over-emphasize the adaptation of organism to environment and the stressful, Spartan efficiency of natural selection — so Veblen along with many other Social Darwinists underestimated man's ability to survive in the face of many unproductive, 'unreasonable' activities. No matter how bounteous the productivity of the 19th century — a century which in the West seemed to want to prove Malthus wrong — Veblen seems to have strongly felt the precariousness of existence, and hence held a tragic view of the consequences of productivity.

Veblen saw history as a process by which man, through workmanship, at long last created the surplus wealth which made him for the first time moderately secure on the earth. But this same surplus, like Eden's apple, permitted a group of new, self-regarding motives to come into being. Emulation entered: men found their pleasure in invidious distinctions at the expense of others. The primitive balance of production and consumption gave way, in Veblen's view, to a world which by his time consisted on the one hand of countries like Germany and Japan where 'too much' productivity put a military surplus in the hands of bellicose dynasts, and on the other of countries like England and America where 'too much' consumption involved all classes of society in a meaningless chase of superfluities for emulative display. In either case, as he was wont to put it, the common man paid the cost.

Now it was paradoxical for Veblen to deplore man's advance beyond the struggle for sheer survival. For the whole point of the activist psychology, as developed by Peirce (under whom Veblen had studied at Hopkins), Dewey and William James, was to lay stress on man's free will and capacity for self-development. Veblen, moreover, had begun by interpreting adaptation as adaptation of the environment to human activity, rather than the reverse. In his first published essay, 'Kant's Critique of Judgment' (1884), he paraphrased Kant as follows: since the knowledge provided the human organism by its perception is fragmentary and unorganized, the organism, which at any given moment is acting as a whole in one or another direction, *adapts* its perceived knowledge into an organized whole: 'the principle of adaptation says that the particular things do belong together, and sets the mind hunting to find out how.'

But Veblen does not fully share James' muscular, unruly sense of human freedom (nor the excesses of James' moral athleticism); to the extent that he does, he is afraid of what men do with their arbitrary power. And so his apparently whole-hearted acceptance of the Jamesian psychology is always qualified and finally overborne by the desire to bind men to a minimal, near-biological routine, in which, if nothing spectacular is accomplished (except in the harmless, out-of-the-way paths of idle learning) no great destruction is wrought either.

Similar fears seem to govern Veblen's attitude toward the joy of work. He shared William Morris' feeling that work should be a central and delightful activity: in *The Theory of the Leisure Class* he speaks of 'the impulse of self-expression and workmanship' (p. 356), and in his essay on 'The Instinct of Workmanship and the Irksomeness of Labour' he attempts to refute the opinion that it is natural for men to look on work as disagreeable by showing how invidious cultural definitions of work as demeaning lead men actually to feel it as such. Moreover, in various places and particularly at the end of *The Instinct of Workmanship*, Veblen states in the strongest terms that human nature is not suited to machine industry, having been genetically fixed in the vastly different societies of prehistory. And yet it is hard to think of a writer who has done more to domesticate the machine, or who has welcomed it with more enthusiasm as a tutor which will make men sober, factual, and peaceable. It would appear, taking all of Veblen's work together, that he regarded the machine as compelling an orientation to the external environment, impersonal as nature itself, capable of creating in men a 'second nature' entirely methodical and workmanlike, rid of the exuberant animistic projections that might be stimulated by more creative or more artisan-like work. Men would suffer under this tutelage, but they would be safe. They would be led back, by a new road to the old pre-emulative ways. Indeed, we see here a dialectical mode in Veblen, inconsistent with his conscious anti-Hegelianism and straight-line evolutionism.

It should be clear, however, that there is lacking in Veblen any glorification of the machine — an attitude probably more common among French auto-fans and Italian poets than among Americans. To glorify the machine, in Veblen's eyes, would be to substitute one superstitious animism for another; he wanted machines, like people, to be treated with solicitude, but not looked up to. Veblen wants people to be aware of living in a cold, impersonal world that cares not for their hopes and responds not to their anthropomorphisms. But again without glory. Machines are machines, nothing more; men are men, nothing more.

Adam Smith had worried in one way about the consequences of mechanized work for the individual; Carlyle, Butler, Ruskin had worried in still other ways; few sensitive intellectuals have been less worried than Veblen.

For one thing, as a farm boy he did not look back on hand labour with nostalgia; for another, he did not have a very exalted idea of what life could be like at best — he himself asked for little enough. But whatever the personal sources of his view, it was productive and challenging to insist that machine work, while it may go against the instinctual grain, does not brutalize the worker, but trains him in a mechanistic rather than animistic kind of intelligence. Like his great contemporary Frederick Taylor, he wanted to see means efficiently adapted to ends, without waste motion — and without waste emotion.

THE CONTAMINATION OF THE COMMON MAN

Veblen spoke of mixture and combination of motives as 'contamination' (Freud uses the term 'repression' and 'sublimation' in a similarly loaded way). For the surplus of motives which economic abundance made possible and inevitable was for Veblen, on the whole, a seduction.

The analysis of contamination is chiefly worked out in connection with the instinct of workmanship — the most diffuse, generalized, and plastic of Veblen's instincts. The parallel transformations of idle curiosity are, by and large, treated as mere reflections of changes in occupational discipline. For instance, the world outlook of early modern times, according to Veblen, expressed the work experience of the hand craftsman who acquires 'natural rights' by mixing his labour with nature's raw materials, and whose God likewise shapes his raw material, the universe, towards self-willed ends. Indeed, Veblen's understanding of the ways in which technology develops out of animism and then turns against it is very suggestive. In *The Instinct of Workmanship* he describes how primitive man, by unscientifically assuming the nature of plants and animals to be like his own, gained a measure of real understanding; that is, his first technology came about through animistic identifications. But as this technology developed, it became increasingly matter-of-fact until it came to constitute in itself an 'environment' which demanded impersonal adaptation for its mastery. The ever-present pressure to be serviceable, which is one aspect of the instinct of workmanship, thus led men by a roundabout route from lore to science, forcing men away from their original animistically guided technology to a mechanistically guided one.

In another sense, of a bent towards craft for craft's sake, the instinct of workmanship is contaminated by emulation, technology's Manichæan foil. In Veblen's view the earliest societies, small and workmanlike, proffered prestige only for particular pieces of work, and to the man who made them only insofar as he was a workman. But as society became larger and private property made its appearance, workmanship was subordinated in two ways. In the first place — so Veblen tells the story — in a large society people could not know intimately each one of their fellow-citizens, so that in place of an appreciation for the actual work a man had done, some more external valuation had to be substituted; in modern society money, the ostensible end of work, and the goods which money will buy, serve this purpose. But this meant that a man's prestige no longer lay in his specialized capacity as a worker, but that a general potency was attributed to him; this attitude was sedulously cultivated by those who, through force and fraud, came to form a ruling class, and reached its full flowering in the concept of the divine right of kings. Beyond this, according to Veblen, there was a second factor working to put down workmanship in its old-fashioned and homely functioning; the incoming of private property and economic inequality placed a prestige value upon leisure, as a symbol of wealth, and work was correspondingly denigrated. That is, Veblen saw the origin of the leisure class in the possibilities for falsification and myth-making offered by bigness, by populations of a certain size, and in the possibilities of aggrandizement and escape from toil provided by private property.

In leisure-class society, however, workmanship is not simply subordinate to emulative uses of leisure, but persists in a perverted (contaminated) form. For, as some faint sense of the serviceable bearing of workmanship still persists in the not completely myth-ridden underlying population, the wasters of the leisure class must deck out their wastemanship as somehow useful to the community at large. Further, the craftsman's feeling for purposeful accomplishment conditions even the pursuit of waste, which is entered upon with a grim efficiency. As Veblen wrote in *The Theory of the Leisure Class* (p. 33):

> That propensity for purposeful activity and that repugnance to all futility of effort which belong to man by virtue of his character as an agent do not desert him when he emerges from the naive communal culture where the dominant mode of life is the unanalyzed and undifferentiated solidarity of the individual with the group with which his livelihood is bound up . . . Under the regime of individual ownership the most available means of visibly achieving a purpose is that afforded by the acquisition and accumulation of goods . . . the propensity for achievement — the instinct of workmanship — tends more and more to shape itself into a straining to excel others in pecuniary achievement.

We can go so far as to say that much of Veblen's work consists of an effort to examine physical artifacts, systems of thought, and individual lives in order to see the interplay of instinctual motives 'frozen' in them, much as Freud saw a physical symptom as the frozen evidence of a psychological conflict. Thus, Veblen looks at classical economic theory to disengage its workmanship from its more or less elegant wastemanship, or he looks with quizzical wonder at the British or American gentleman, with his ability to be brilliantly incompetent in all industrial matters, effortfully idle, and calculatingly extravagant. Still again he will make what we might term a 'content analysis' of particular objects in search of workmanship entwined with waste; as he writes (in *The Theory of the Leisure Class*, pp. 100-101):

> Even in articles which seem at first glance to serve for pure ostentation only, it is always possible to detect the pretence of some, at least ostensible, useful purpose; and on the other hand, even in special machinery and tools contrived for some particular industrial process, as well as in the rudest appliances of human industry, the traces of conspicuous waste, or at least of the habit of ostentation, usually become evident on a close scrutiny.

This 'content analysis' of objects and theories quite obviously proceeds on the basis of a theory of unconscious motivation in their human makers and users. Men, according to Veblen, conceal for themselves what they feel and do: they rationalize as decorously wasteful the activities that actually serve the common good, for to be useful has often become as demeaning as being 'in trade' once was.

Conversely, the perhaps more typically, they find some utility, even necessity, in actions that serve primarily to keep them in the pecuniary race of intrepid expenditure or the occupational race of avoiding work of servile imputation. That they do this, even when the activity in question appears senseless to the culturally insensitive eye, testifies in Veblen's judgment to the strength of the human propensity to lead a meaningful existence. In other words, rationalization is the ever-recurring symptom of our desire to be reasonable. In seeing that the collision between human instincts and cultural pressures produced compromises both in motivation and action, Veblen was working in the spirit of the discoveries in the field of psychoanalysis that Freud was simultaneously making. In fact, whereas Freud tended to assume that the latent, the hidden motive was the real McCoy, Veblen had a less dogmatic view of the process of disentangling a mixture of motives: it was in each case a question of evidence to determine whether the overt or the latent factors predominated, and things might occasionally be what they seemed.

David Riesman

(This is the first of two instalments of Dr. Riesman's article on Veblen. The second will appear in our next number.)

CUSTOMS OF MAJORCA

The Balearics — Majorca, Iviza and Minorca with several smaller islands — lie in a fine-weather area, a night's sail to the east of Barcelona. Agriculturalists from Libya colonized Majorca, the largest of the group, about the middle of the second millennium B.C., and Cyclopean round towers called *talayots* survive from this time, mainly in the southern plain. A later type of *talayot* is square, and built with smaller stones. The island was of outstanding importance in the Bronze Age, being the nearest source of tin for the Cretans and Mycenaeans, who extracted from it the lead mined at Buñola, one of the few mountain-sites where *talayots* occur. Their maritime successors, the Rhodians, are said by Strabo to have colonized the island after the Fall of Troy. Silius Italicus, a Spanish poet, mentions Tleptolemus the Rhodian, who brought nine ships to the siege of Troy, as having landed here with his comrade Lindus.

Next, the Phoenicians recruited Balearic slingers for their armies from the whole group of islands, founded Mago (now Port Mahon in Minorca) and made Iviza their national necropolis. They did not hold Majorca in strength, and left few relics of their stay apart from the great gift of olive oil; it was they who taught the islanders how to graft the true olive on the oleaster and who set up oil-mills. The island had long repudiated its allegiance to Carthage when the Romans conquered it under Q. Caecilius Metellus in 123 B.C., founded the cities of Palma, Pollensa and Sineu, and enlisted the slingers in their own armies. For accuracy of aim, shaped leaden sling-bolts – some of them stamped with the letters BAL – were now preferred to stones, and Ovid writes hyperbolically in his *Metamorphoses* that they flew at such speed as to melt the air.

The two most important Classical sources for native customs in Majorca are Diodorus Siculus and Strabo.

Diodorus writes:

There are other islands over against Spain, which the Grecians call Gymnesiae, because in summer-time the inhabitants go naked. By the natives and the Romans they are called Baleares, from casting of huge massy stones out of slings, wherein the inhabitants excel all other people. The greater of these islands is larger than all the rest of the islands, except these seven, Sicily, Sardinia, Cyprus, Crete, Euboea, Corsica and Lesbos. It is only a day's sail distant from Spain. The lesser lies more eastward, and breeds and feeds all sorts of fine and large cattle, especially mules, which for the bigness of their bodies, and the exceeding noise they make in their braying, are remarkable above all others. Both these islands are of good and fertile soil, and are peopled with about thirty thousand inhabitants.

As to the fruits of the earth, they are altogether destitute of wine; the want therefore of it makes them the more eager after it. Neither have they any oil amongst them; to supply which, they press out the oily part of mastic, and mix it and swine's grease together, and with this composition anoint their bodies.

They love women exceedingly, whom they value at such a rate that when the pirates bring any women they have taken thither, they will give as a ransom, three or four men for one woman. They live in caves hewn in the rocks, and spend all their days in these holes, dug up and down in the steepest part of the rocky mountains, by which means they provide for themselves both shelter and security.

They make no use either of silver or gold coin, but prohibit the importation of it into the island; for which they give this reason: that Hercules, in former times, made war upon Geryon the son of Chrysaor, for no other reason but because he was rich in silver, gold and, therefore, that they may live more securely, and quietly enjoy what they have, they have made it a standing law to have nothing to do with wealth which consists in those metals. According, therefore, to this decree, when once heretofore in a war they assisted the Carthaginians, they brought nothing of their pay into their own country, but laid it all out in wine and women.

They have a filthy custom likewise amongst them concerning their marriages; for in their marriage-feasts, all their friends and household servants, as they are in seniority of age, one after another, carnally know the bride, till at length it comes to the bridegroom's turn, who has the honour to be last.

They have another strange custom likewise about burying of their dead; they cut the carcase in pieces with wooden knives or axes, and so put up all the parts into an urn, and then raise up a great heap of stones over it.

Their arms are three slings, one they wind about their heads, another they tie about their loins, and the third they carry in their hands. In time of war they throw much larger stones than any other people and with that violence, as if they were shot out of an engine; and, therefore, in the time of assaults made upon towns, they grievously gall those that stand upon the bulwarks and in field-fights break in pieces their enemies' shields, helmets, and all other defensive armour whatsoever; and are such exact marksmen, (that for the most part) they never miss what they aim at: they attain this skill by continual exercise from their very childhood; for while they are very young, they are forced, under the tutorage of their mothers, to cast stones out of slings. For they fasten a piece of bread for a mark to a pole, and till the child hit the bread, he must fast, and then at length the mother gives him the bread to eat.

To this Strabo adds:

The larger of the Gymnasiae contains two cities, Palma and Polentia; the latter lying towards the east, the former towards the west. The length of this island is scarcely less than 600 stadia, its breadth 200; although Artemidorus asserts it is twice this size both in length and breadth. The smaller island is about 270 stadia distant from Polentia; in size it is far surpassed by the larger island, but in excellence it is by no means inferior, for both of them are very fertile, and furnished with harbours. At the mouths of these however they are rocks rising but a little out of the water, which renders attention necessary in entering them. The fertility of these places inclines the inhabitants to peace, as also the people of Ebusus (Iviza). But certain malefactors, though few in number, having associated with the pirates in those seas, they all got a bad name, and Metellus, surnamed Balearicus, marched against them. He it was who built the cities. But owing to the great fertility of the country, these people have always had enemies plotting against them. Although naturally disposed to peace, they bear the reputation of being most excellent slingers, which art they have been most proficient in since the time that the Phoenicians possessed the islands. It is said that these were the first who introduced amongst the men the custom of wearing tunics with wide borders. They were accustomed to go into battle naked, having a shield covered with goat-skin in their hand, and a javelin hardened by fire at the point, very rarely with an iron tip, and wearing around the head three slings of black rush, hair or sinew. The long sling they use for hitting at far distances, the short one for near marks, and the middle one for those between. From childhood they were so thoroughly practised in the use of slings, that bread was never distributed to the children till they had won it by the sling. On this account Metellus, when he was approaching the islands, spread pelts over the decks, as a shelter from the slings. He introduced into the country 3000 Roman colonists from Spain.

In addition to the fruitfulness of the land, noxious animals are rarely to be met with. Even the rabbits, they say, were not indigenous, but that a male and female having been introduced by some one from the opposite continent, from thence the whole stock sprung, which formerly was so great a nuisance that even houses and trees were overturned, being undermined by their warrens, and the inhabitants were compelled, as we have related, to resort for refuge to the Romans. However, at the present day the facility with which these animals are taken, prevents them from doing injury, consequently those who possess land cultivate it with advantage. These islands are on this side of what are called the Pillars of Hercules.

* * *

To summarize briefly the subsequent history of Majorca. A number of Jews arrived from Rome about 50 A.D., after their expulsion by Claudius, and seem to have been joined by refugees from Palestine after the Fall of Jerusalem, and again after Bar Cochba's revolt in 132 A.D. The Jews form one of the main racial elements in the population. In the fifth century came the Vandals of Carthage. In the sixth, Belisarius recovered the island for 'Rome', which meant Byzantium, Rome being then in Ostrogothic hands. Two centuries later, the Moors landed and, except for a temporary occupation by Charlemagne's Franks from 801 to 807, and another by the Pisans, Genoese and Catalans from 1108 to 1114, held the island until 1229, when Jaime I of Aragon restored it to Christendom. It has ever since been in the possession of his royal successors. The Moors were superb husbandmen; they terraced the mountains for olive-culture, built complicated irrigation systems, and founded most of the mountain villages. Their work has been maintained and enlarged; already by 1624 the annual oil yield is said to have exceeded twenty million gallons. But Jaime's men imposed their language which is akin to Provençal, on the islanders, and this is still the vernacular, though all official business is now done in Castilian.

Unfortunately, neither Diodorus nor Strabo being an anthropologist, we cannot decide whether every corpse was mutilated as Diodorus describes, or only the corpse of a chief, or sacrificial victim; whether the cairn served to prevent the ghost from breaking out of the urn, and whether only the extremities of the body were hacked off — as Jason immobilized the ghost of his murdered brother-in-law Apsyrtus at Tomi; or whether the cairn served as an altar, and certain limbs or organs of the body had first been used to blood the new chief — as English children are blooded at their first fox-hunt — and thus imbue him with divinity. It can only be said that, today, Majorcan villagers pay scant attention to a corpse once the requiem mass has been sung, leaving it propped against a wall for the sacristan to bury at leisure, while they return, weeping apotropaically, to the funeral breakfast.

Nor can we be sure whether the 'filthy marriage custom' described by Diodorus was confined to the personage known in Africa as the 'village wife', who becomes the legitimized prostitute of all local bachelors and widowers until she resigns her position and chooses a husband; or whether the Majorcans were polyandrous, like the Libyans of the Lesser Syrtis (Herodotus: iv. 179), and any woman adopting the new custom of monogamy had first to gratify the men whom she was thus depriving of her expected favours. It may therefore be a coincidence, rather than a survival, that nowadays after the wedding breakfast in a mountain village, the bride retires to the bedroom with a large tray which she lays on the bridal bed; whereupon the men of the village file past, beginning with the oldest and gravest, kiss her good luck, and throw money on the tray, while the bridegroom stands sheepishly by.

The Majorcans' regard for women is still profound. A housewife is called '*Sa Madoña*' — almost a divine title — and no male member of the household dares buy a pig, a mule, or a plot of land without consulting her. They justify it biblically with a *refran*, or rhymed proverb, which runs:

Solomon who was very wise
Declared: "One fine day
The women will encompass the men about."
And this has now come to pass.

The fruit-trade of almost all French provincial towns, from Nancy to Nantes, and from Dinant to Perpignan, is monopolized by Majorcans of the mountain villages: it is largely the women's extraordinary energy, courage and business acumen that has made this possible. Tradition relates that during the frequent raids by Barbary pirates, which ceased only in the early 19th century, women took a prominent part in beating off the invaders. History was repeated sixteen years ago, after Captain Bayo's ill-starred landing at Puerto Cristo; the housewives with their pig-killing knives came out against the Catalan and French invaders.

Families are very clannish. Meals are simple: consisting mainly of bread, oil, vegetables, sausage and figs. Houses are uncluttered by furniture and ornaments; children own few toys. Money is respected, but few Majorcans are grasping; and in the villages annual debts are usually called in only on New Year's Day. The safest investment is thought to be real estate; hence land prices bear little relation to the possible agricultural yield of the property sold.

The military importance of slingers began to decline in the 6th century A.D., when Belisarius improved Roman archery by borrowing the Scythian technique of drawing the arrow back to the ear, instead of shooting from the chest in Greek style; until then Balearic slingers outranged the ordinary bowman by twenty or thirty yards and, like the men of Benjamin, could 'sling at a hair'. Slinging is said to have been introduced from Rhodes; and, if so, was not the only Rhodian contribution to island culture. The famous Bronze Age bulls' heads found at Lluchmayor suggest Rhodian inspiration; Rhodes was famous for its sun-bulls sacred to the god Teshub, or Atabyrius. Moreover, the *xiurell*, a white clay whistle handmade by women in traditional shapes – mermaid, mystagogue, serpent, moon-goddess with child, and bull-headed man – decorated with splashes of red and green paint, and blown in Church processions at the time of the September winnowing festival, is distinctly Rhodian in appearance. (This is one of the rare occasions when the sound of a whistle can be heard on Majorca: whistling is believed to raise winds, and 'the farmer's purse hangs on the tree' – the chief riches of the island being now olives, figs and almonds.)

The Balearic slinger is not yet extinct. In remote Majorcan villages, shepherds still carry slings, which they use not only for killing rabbits and birds, but for controlling their flocks. Their aim is uncannily good. Straying goats are checked at long range by a blow on their horns. Forty years ago, slings were in more general use, and a couple of gangsters from Barcelona who tried to hold up the village of Santa Maria had their pistols knocked out of their hands and their skulls smashed, at the entrance to the village, by slingers standing out of effective pistol range. At Galilea, an angry peasant recently broke all the uprights of his employer's garden gate, one after the other, from sixty paces, with twelve successive hits and no misses; and in that neighbourhood slings are still preferred to shotguns for bringing down partridges on the wing. However, the traditional slinging-battles between the *lotes,* or youths, of rival parishes were prohibited by law two generations ago; and in most towns and villages even the small boys have lost their skill. Ceremonial battles took place on Sundays and important feast days, after Mass, across the watercourse which divides Palma and Porto-Pi, while thousands of people looked down from a safe station on the old city walls. Concussions and blindings were frequent and regarded as acts of God. Similar battles between the mountain villages of Bañalbufar and Estellenchs are said to have originated centuries ago in a Sabine Rape of Bañalbufar girls by the *lotes* of Estellenchs. Yet the most striking characteristic of the Majorcans, besides their hospitality and trustworthiness, is still 'their natural disposition to peace,' which Strabo recorded. Crimes of violence are exceptional, and if any occur, it is always said in the cafés: 'What a disgrace! The man must have been an Ivizan, or a foreigner.' Majorcans like to joke about their cowardice, and see no point in going to war except in defence of their own homes; but are skilful sailors and resolute smugglers.

The function of the *lotes,* who correspond with the 'young warrior' group among the Masai and other East African cattle-raising peoples, is to act as village police in cases where the civil law has not been infringed, but tradition or good taste have been flouted — if, for instance, there is too great a disparity between the ages of bride and bridegroom; or if a widow remarries six months after the death of her husband, the shortest time permitted by law; or if a case of cuckoldry has became notorious. They apply sanctions by blowing conches outside the house all night — the conch being otherwise used only to announce the arrival of the fishwives in the village square. There is a strong distaste for drunkenness in the island — a legacy, perhaps from the Moors and Jews — though vines have long been introduced and wines are excellent; the *lotes* are therefore allowed and even encouraged to duck any troublesome drunk in the *picas* — the long stone troughs at which women wash clothes.

If a priest mortally offends a village by some sexual irregularity, or gross interference with custom, the *lotes* will give him increasingly severe warnings. First they assemble in front of the church at Mass-time, and walk away pointedly when he approaches. Should he persist in his shortcomings, they will blow conches outside the rectory for three nights running; and if that has no effect, will undo their trousers, squat solemnly in a row on his doorstep, and excrete. Since a priest's person is sacrosanct, he cannot be thrown into the *picas*; and what they would do to him next, I daresay, would be what is done to a woman who has disgraced her village — for women are equally sacrosanct. About twenty-five years ago a woman murdered her husband, and came home from prison after seven years to resume her former life. That night the *lotes* securely boarded up her doors and first-storey windows, leaving her to face starvation. But since the Majorcans are not a cruel people — they seldom beat their children or animals — someone set a ladder against an upper window; which enabled her to escape unmolested with whatever goods she could carry away in a bundle. This technique has also been noted in the Cameroons, where the boarding-up is done by women.

The advantage of leaving such police duties to the *lotes* is that adults do not become involved in family feuds, court cases, or trouble with the Church. In theory, the *lotes* are irresponsible members of society: therefore, should the Bishop send his Chaplain to enquire why Father Fullano has been insulted, the mayor will smile and say: '*Ka,* (a contemptuous disclaimer) that is a matter of the *lotes!* Pray do not take it seriously. I know nothing about it.' But in all likelihood the mayor himself has said: 'This disagreeable situation cannot continue; now, when I was a *lot* . . . ' About seventy years ago the *lotes* of Fornalutx drove out a scandalously living priest; and the village was put to great inconvenience by being left priestless for some years. The *lotes* frequently club together to hire a bus or car for a 'bullfight' in Palma; though their main intention is to visit the brothels. '*Ka* — a matter of the *lotes!* Let them do what they like away from home, so long as they behave decently here.'

It is a long-established moral axiom in the villages that nobody steals from his neighbour. Doors are not normally locked at night, and if a family absents itself from home by day, the key is trustingly left in the front door lock — unless gipsies or Catalans happen to be about. Fruit-trees are respected, though if one visits relatives and finds them away, one may pick a few almonds or apricots by virtue of kinship; but not fill a basket. It is also a tradition that the *lotes* may come by night to rob the melon-patch of the mayor or principal landowner. Twenty years ago, when I first built a house and bought land in the village of Deyá, I did not realize that I was being paid a backhanded compliment when I found my melons stolen; the then mayor not having planted any. For a few centimos the *lotes* could have bought a melon in the village shop, and mine were not yet ripe; but the custom — paralleled by similar yam-stealing in the South Seas — had to be maintained. When I come to think of it, several years have passed since the *lotes* of Deyá have played their traditional rôle as moral police. Probably, because under the present Government our seven village coastguards have been converted into armed police — before the Civil War our police station was eight miles away — and the task of keeping law and order is now officially committed to their charge.

Girls and boys cease playing with each other at the age of five or six, and will not meet socially until they start 'talking', which means walking out, at the age of sixteen or seventeen. On Sundays and feastdays, *taringes,* or arm-in-arm bands, either of girls or of boys belonging to the same age-group, walk up and down the village street dressed in their best clothes. The encounter between *taringes* of the opposite sex is mildly exciting, since covert glances are exchanged between couples who will eventually pair off and 'talk' — but not yet. And once a couple has paired off, it is three chances to one that they will remain so paired until death parts them. Not long ago a man from Deyá who had lived in Cuba for thirty years, brought back his family. His daughters complained bitterly that the young men with whom they walked out never once mentioned love, beauty, adventure, or anything interesting, and talked of nothing but the weather, the olive harvest, and commodity prices. Pre-nuptial intercourse in the village is exceptional and, if detected, almost always followed by a wedding; since a girl cannot hope to marry if she is known to have slept with anyone except her future husband. A girl disgraced by an affair with a married man, if she cannot move away, is likely to become an unofficial 'village wife' and, perhaps, when she grows older, a witch. Witches are still active and much consulted, despite all efforts of the Church. They secure abortions, sell love-philtres and *mal bossis,* or death-charms, and lift spells cast by other witches. Santa Catalina, the red-light district of Palma, is their centre, and they claim to have a Bishop who directs them from the Puerto Rican section in New York.

In the villages the Church condemns but cannot altogether suppress, ballroom dancing *(baile agarado)* introduced from France; it encourages folk-dancing, in which a couple's only contact is between their finger tips. Recently at Deyá, the Priest went into a café where a dance was in progress and hauled out all girls under sixteen. No sanctions were taken against him by the *lotes;* it was felt that he had acted with his rights.

The nearest approach to full-blooded love-making comes with the *matanza,* the autumn killing and disposal of the family pig, to which members of several other households are invited in the confidence of return invitations. Broad jokes are permitted on such occasions. The pig is jointed, its flesh, ground up and mixed with *pimiento,* becomes red sausage, its bones are salted down, the hams hung up the chimney, the blood made into black pudding and black sausage. No menstruating woman may attend, because her presence would turn the meat. The liver, brains, kidneys and similar offal, which will be the reward of the sausage-makers, are always laid out on carob branches; which is puzzling at first, like the custom of separating men and women in church. The women enter by the main door and sit in the rear; the men enter by a side-door and sit in front. But this is a Jewish custom designed to protect the men: since a menstruous woman passing between two of them would, according to the Mishna, endanger life. Nearly all Majorcan Jews became Christians after Jaime I's conquest. Those who stood by their faith, mainly the goldsmiths' guild, were forcibly converted, or burned, under Philip II; when, to avoid pogroms, the converts used to sit in their shop windows ostentatiously chewing a pork chop — hence their nickname *chu' eta.* But a feeling of guilt lingered among them, and may well account for the propitiatory carob branches at the *matanzas,* the *carob* being a Hebrew symbol of repentance — the Prodigal Son in the parable repents of his evil deeds and his herding of unclean swine when he eats 'husks', namely the carob-beans.

'Eyes' painted in whitewash around the windows of older houses have been explained as discouraging rats from climbing in, but are, rather, a relic of the Moorish period: a charm against the evil eye. When, or by whom, the custom was originated of whitewashing a house throughout after a member of the family has died there, I cannot say; but this is done even if a death occurs immediately after the Spring whitewashing, and even if it has not been caused by a contagious disease. Psychologically, this custom is most valuable: since it distracts the bereaved women by making them work hard, with the help of neighbours or relations. Perhaps its origin is Jewish, again: the Jews would whitewash their sepulchres to put a protective layer of chalk between the unclean stone and anyone who might inadvertently touch it.

Robert Graves

STRESS

In this article I discuss biologic stress from two points of view. First, I summarize the basic observations that led to the evolution of the stress concept.[1] Second, I attempt to formulate – in a manner necessarily subjective – the relationship between specific and non-specific actions, which I consider the most prominent aspect of future stress research.

1

Ever since man used the word 'disease' or its equivalent, he has had some inkling of the stress concept. The very fact that a great variety of maladies can be denoted by a single term indicates they have something in common. They possess, as we would now say, some non-specific features which distinguish disease from health. Yet because these manifestations are not characteristic of any one disease, they have received little attention in comparison with specific ones. They attracted less interest, for, unlike the latter, they neither helped in the recognition of the 'eliciting pathogen' nor lent themselves to specific therapy.

---

[1] For an analysis of the literature on biologic stress, see H. Selye, 'Stress. The physiology and pathology of exposure to systemic stress.' 1950, and 'First annual report on stress.' 1951; H. Selye and A. Horava, 'Second annual report on stress.' 1952, and 'Third annual report on stress.' 1953; and H. Selye, 'The story of the adaptation syndrome.' 1952.

The experimental work upon which this survey is based has been subsidized, in part, by a consolidated research grant of the National Research Council of Canada.

Nevertheless, several early investigators attempted to elucidate the mechanisms involved in such non-specific reactions. Since our knowledge of the nervous system antedates by far the development of modern endocrinology, it is understandable that the former was the first to be examined from this point of view. Ricker, Speransky, Reilly, Hoff and many others gathered data concerning the role of the nervous system in such non-specific reactions as fever, polymorphonuclear leucocytosis, inflammation, etc. In the field of physiologic stress, Cannon clarified the role of the sympathetic nervous system and its humoral effector substances. And quite independently, progress was made in the study of pituitary and adreno-cortical hormones by chemists, physiologists and clinicians, too numerous to mention.

The knowledge thus acquired was indispensable in the formulation of the stress concept as a unifying principle. Additional experiments showed that the many non-specific responses of individual target organs were closely integrated, representing part of a single biologic response – the adaptation syndrome – and playing an integrated part in the most varied physiologic, pathologic and pharmacologic reactions.

Experimental work in animals (1936), demonstrated that the organism responds in a stereotyped manner to a variety of factors such as infections, intoxications, trauma, nervous strain, heat, cold, muscular fatigue or x-irradiation. The specific actions of these agents were quite different. Their only common feature was that they placed the body in a state of general (systemic) stress. We therefore concluded that this stereotyped response, which was superimposed upon the specific effects, represented the somatic manifestations of non-specific stress itself.

But what is 'non-specific stress'? In physics the word denotes the interaction between a force and the resistance opposed to it, for example, pressure and tension putting inanimate matter under stress. The non-specific response is thought to be the biologic equivalent of physical stress, and today the term is widely accepted in this sense.

GENERAL ADAPTATION SYNDROME (G-A-S)

The outstanding manifestations of this stress response were (1) adreno-cortical enlargement with histologic signs of hyperactivity, (2) thymico-lymphatic involution with certain concomitant changes in the blood-count and (3) gastrointestinal ulcers, often accompanied by other manifestations of damage or shock. We were struck by the fact that during this reaction, although all organs in the body showed involutional or degenerative changes, the adrenal cortex actually seemed to flourish on stress. We suspected this adrenal response played a useful part in a non-specific adaptive reaction — a call to arms of the body's defence forces — and named it the 'alarm reaction'. Subsequent studies showed that the alarm reaction was the first stage of a prolonged general adaptation syndrome. The latter comprised three distinct stages: (1) the alarm reaction in which adaptation had not yet been acquired; (2) the stage of resistance, in which adaptation was optimal; and (3) the stage of exhaustion, in which the acquired adaptation was lost again.

To elucidate the kinetics of this syndrome, rats were adrenalectomized and then exposed to stressor agents. This showed that in the absence of the adrenals, stress could no longer cause thymico-lymphatic involution or the characteristic blood-count changes. When adrenalectomized rats were treated with the impure cortical extracts available at that time, it became evident that thymico-lymphatic involution and typical blood-count changes could be produced by adrenal hormones even in the absence of the adrenals. The latter, therefore, were considered indirect results of stress mediated by corticoids.

Conversely, gastrointestinal ulcers and other manifestations of pure damage or shock were more severe in adrenalectomized animals than in intact ones and could be lessened by treatment with cortical extracts. It was concluded that these lesions were not mediated through the adrenal, but were combated by an adequate adreno-cortical response to stressor agents.

But what stimulated adreno-cortical function during stress? In 1937 we found that among many surgical interventions tried, only hypophysectomy prevented the adrenal response during the alarm reaction. Hence we concluded that stress stimulated the cortex through an adreno-corticotrophic hormone, now known as ACTH.

Then pure cortical steroids became available, thanks first to the investigations of Kendall and Reichstein. With these we could show that the administration of mineralo-corticoids or M-Cs, such as desoxycorticosterone, produced experimental replicas of the so-called hypersensitive and inflammatory 'rheumatic' diseases: notably, nephrosclerosis, hypertension, vascular lesions (especially periarteritis nodosa and hyalin necrosis of arterioles), as well as arthritic changes resembling, in acute experiments, those of rheumatic fever and, after chronic treatment, those of rheumatoid arthritis. Yet even very high doses of mineralo-corticoids did not induce noteworthy thymico-lymphatic or blood-count changes. Furthermore, exposure of animals to non-specific stressor agents (e.g., cold) produced marked adreno-cortical enlargement and organ changes very similar to those elicited by the administration of mineralo-corticoids.

Gluco-corticoids (G-Cs) such as cortisone, on the other hand, were highly potent in causing thymico-lymphatic involution and in eliciting the characteristic blood-count changes of the alarm reaction. They also tended to inhibit the hypertensive and rheumatic changes which could be elicited in animals by mineralo-corticoids. In these respects the two types of corticoid hormones antagonized each other.

The terms 'gluco-corticoids' and 'mineralo-corticoids' emphasize the salient metabolic actions of these changes. From the clinical point of view, however, their effects upon inflammation are perhaps of greater interest. Since the gluco-corticoids inhibit inflammation, while the mineralo-corticoids enhance it, the G-Cs may appropriately be called antiphlogistic or A-Cs and the M-Cs, prophlogistic corticoids, or P-Cs when discussed with reference to their effects upon inflammation.

Inflammatory granulomas, especially those produced in the vicinity of the joints by the local application of irritants (e.g., formalin, mustard powder), as well as certain allergic reactions, were likewise aggravated by P-Cs and inhibited by A-Cs. Apparently the response of the adrenal cortex was important not only in defence against systemic stress affecting the whole organism, but also in the manifold topical defence reactions which occurred upon exposure to local stress.

Certain crude anterior-pituitary extracts duplicated these actions of P-Cs upon the cardiovascular system, the blood pressure, the connective tissue (inflammation), and the kidneys. The hypophyseal preparations which we used were definitely corticotrophic since they enlarged the adrenal cortex, but they were particularly rich in the somatotrophic or growth hormone, STH. As soon as we were able to obtain purified ACTH, it became evident that such pathogenic actions of crude anterior-pituitary preparations could not be due to their ACTH content, since even the highest tolerable doses of the latter failed to duplicate their predominant P-C effects. On the other hand, overdosage with pure STH caused cardiovascular and renal lesions identical with those previously observed in animals treated with P-Cs. It was concluded that the actions of our crude anterior-pituitary preparations were mainly due to their STH content. It remains to be seen to what extent STH acts indirectly by stimulating the P-C production of the adrenal cortex or directly by sensitizing the peripheral tissues to M-Cs. Preliminary observations suggest that both mechanisms are implicated, but the point is still in doubt.

From the internists' point of view, perhaps the most interesting role of STH in the adaptation syndrome is that it can effectively combat catabolism and susceptibility to infections. Animals heavily overdosed with ACTH or A-Cs tend to lose a great deal of weight. Eventually they die, almost always as a result of generalized septicemia caused by normally saprophytic micro-organisms. In rats the lung tissue appears to be singularly predisposed to such infections. Under these conditions, adequate doses of STH prevent loss of body weight as well as excessive microbial proliferation. It remains to be seen to what extent these STH actions will prove of value in the management of human infections, but experiments on rats have already demonstrated the great influence of these hormones upon resistance to the human type of tuberculosis. Normally the rat is virtually resistant to tuberculosis bacilli; it may be rendered sensitive by ACTH or A-Cs and this sensitivity in turn can be abolished by STH.

As work progressed, it became obvious that the activity of hormones produced during stress depended largely upon a variety of conditioning factors. Both the production of the adaptive hormones and their effect upon individual target organs proved to be greatly influenced by heredity, previous exposure to stress, nutritional state, etc. Thus the production of corticotrophic hormone by the pituitary was enhanced by a high-protein diet, while the action of M-Cs upon most target organs was augmented by excess sodium.

Stress itself was perhaps the most effective and most common factor capable of conditioning the actions of adaptive hormones. Thus systemic stress augmented the lympholytic, catabolic and hyperglycemic actions of G-Cs, while the salient effect of the adaptive hormones, that of modifying the course of inflammation, naturally could not manifest itself unless some topical stressor first elicited a phlogistic response.

In any last analysis, such factors determined whether exposure to stressor agents would be met by a physiologic G-A-S or would cause 'diseases of adaptation'. Indeed, in the latter instance these conditioning factors appeared responsible for the selective breakdown of one organ rather than another. We felt that differences in predisposition might explain why the same kind of stress could cause diverse types of diseases of adaptation in different individuals.

It was concluded from these experiments that the pathogenicity of many systemic and local stressor agents depended largely upon the function of the hypophysis-adreno-cortical system. The latter might either enhance or inhibit the body's defence reactions against stressor agents. We thought derailments of this adaptive mechanism were the principal factors in the production of certain maladies which might therefore be considered diseases of adaptation.

Among the derailments of the G-A-S which might cause disease, the following proves important: (1) absolute excess or deficiency in corticoids and STH produced during stress; (2) absolute excess or deficiency in corticoids and STH retained or 'fixed' by their principal target organs during stress; (3) disposition in the relative secretion or fixation during stress of ACTH and A-Cs, on the one hand, and of STH and P-Cs on the other; (4) production by stress of metabolic derangements which abnormally altered the target organ's response to STH, ACTH or corticoids through the phenomenom of 'conditioning'; (5) and finally, though the hypothysis-adrenal mechanism played a prominent role in the G-A-S, other organs might also respond abnormally and become the cause of disease during adaptation to stress.

All agents, then, which act upon the body or any of its parts exert dual effects: specific actions, and non-specific or stressor effects. The principal pathways of the latter, as far as we know them today, are illustrated in Figure 1. Note that the stressor acts upon the target (the body or some part of it) directly (thick arrow) and indirectly through the pituitary and adrenal. Through some unknown pathway (question mark), the 'first mediator' travels from the directly injured area to the anterior pituitary. It notifies the latter that a condition of stress exists and thus induces it to discharge ACTH. It is possible this first mediator is not always the same. In some instances, it may be an adrenaline discharge, in others a liberation of histamine-like toxic tissue metabolites, a nervous impulse, or even a sudden deficiency in some vital body constituent such as glucose or an enzyme.

ACTH stimulates the adrenal cortex to discharge corticoids. Some of these, the prophlogistic corticoids, stimulate the proliferative ability and reactivity of connective tissue; they enhance the inflammatory potential and thus help put up a barricade of connective tissue through which the body is protected against further invasion by the pathogenic stressor agent. However, under ordinary conditions, ACTH stimulates the adrenal much more effectively to secrete antiphlogistic corticoids. These inhibit the ability of the body to put up granulomatous barricades in the path of the invader; in fact, they tend to cause involution of connective tissue with a pronounced depression of the inflammatory potential and thus open the way for the spread of infection.

As far as we know, ACTH always stimulates the adrenal to produce various corticoids in the same proportion and always with a great predominance of A-Cs. However, STH also increases the inflammatory potential of connective tissue somewhat as the P-Cs do and hence sensitizes the target area to the actions of the latter.

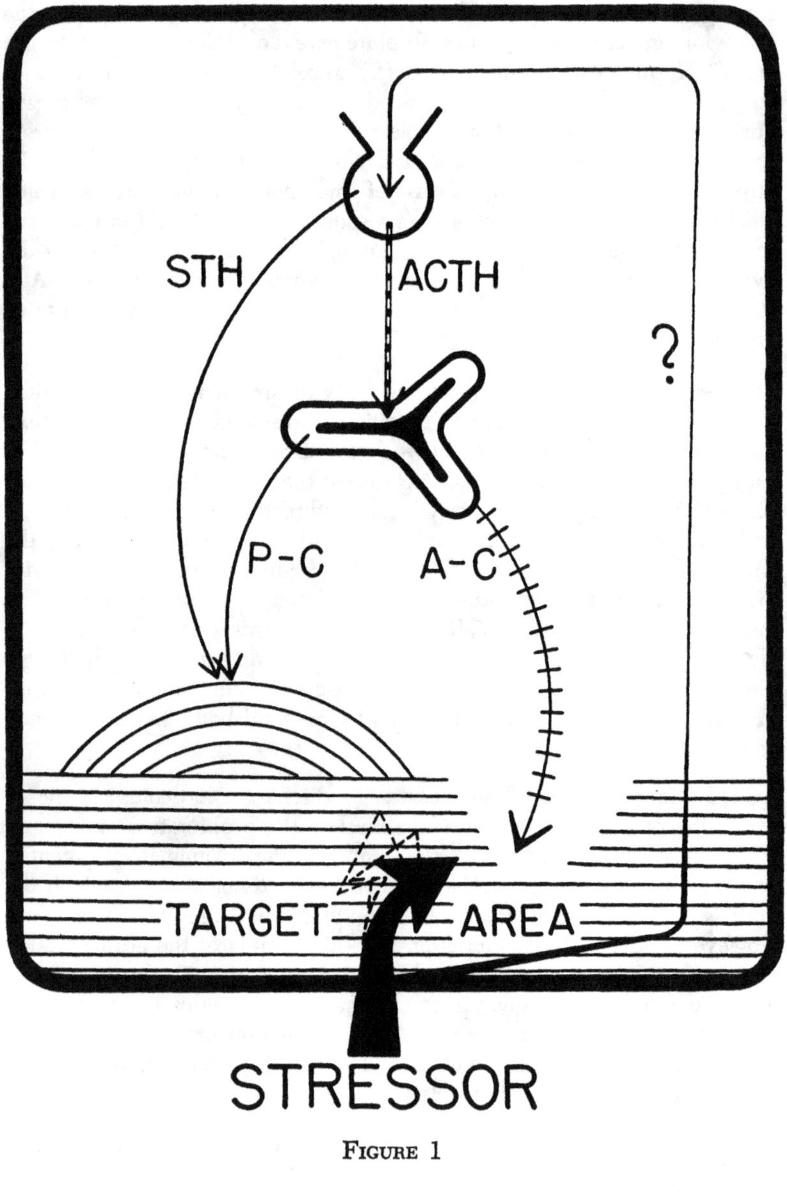

FIGURE 1

It is possible that the hypophysis also secretes some special corticotrophin which induces the adrenal to elaborate predominantly P-Cs; indeed, STH itself may possess such effects, but this has not yet been proven. In any event, if ACTH were the only corticotrophin, the actions of the corticoids produced under its influence would be vastly different, depending upon conditioning factors such as STH which specifically sensitize the target area for one or the other type of corticoid action. Actually, conditioning factors might even alter the response to ACTH of the adrenal cortex itself, so that its cells would produce more A-Cs or P-Cs. Thus, during stress, one or the other type of effect can predominate.

The fundamental reaction-pattern to topical stressors is a local adaptation syndrome with inflammation, to systemic stressors, the general adaptation syndrome. Various combinations of these two basic responses constitute the essence of most diseases.

Pasteur and his contemporaries introduced the concept of specificity into medicine. The theory which directed their fruitful investigations held that the organism could develop specific adaptive reactions against individual pathogens and that by imitating and complementing these, wherever short of optimal, many diseases due to specific pathogens could be treated.

The G-A-S, on the other hand, holds that many diseases have no single cause — no specific pathogen — but are largely due to non-specific stress and to pathogenic situations which result from inappropriate responses to such non-specific stress. It seems to me, if I may reiterate an opinion, that research on stress will be most fruitful if it is guided by the theory that we must learn to imitate — if necessary to correct and complement — the body's own auto-pharmacologic efforts to combat the stress factor in disease.

2

The general and local adaptation syndromes have already been discussed as stress reactions. Since the latter has only recently been described in detail[1], Figure 2, which summarizes its characteristic features, is given. The relationship between these two syndromes is worth reviewing. Both are non-specific reactions comprising damage and defence. Both are triphasic with typical signs of 'crossed resistance' or, depending upon the stressors used, 'crossed sensitization' during the second stage. Both are singularly sensitive to adaptive hormones (ACTH, STH, corticoids). If developed simultaneously in the same individual, each greatly influences

[1] H. Selye, 'The part of inflammation in the local adaptation syndrome.' in *Symposium on the Mechanism of Inflammation*, eds. G. Jasmin and A. Robert, 1953.

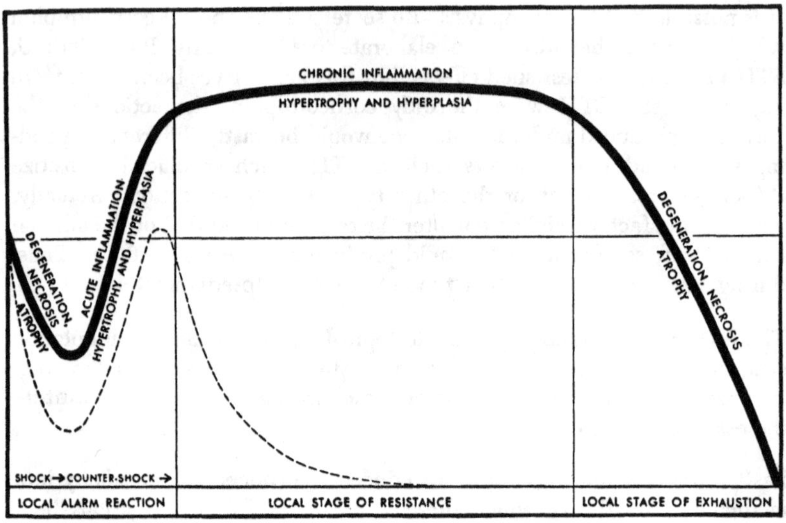

FIGURE 2

the other; that is, systemic stress markedly alters tissue-reactivity to local stress and vice versa.

In our earliest studies on systemic stress, the phenomena of crossed resistance and cross sensitization were observed. Later it was possible to characterize them with greater precision by using the granuloma technique.[1] It will be recalled that the granuloma pouch technique is based upon the possibility of sharply delimiting an area of connective tissue by subcutaneous insufflation of air. One can then inject a local stressor (e.g., croton oil, mustard powder, formalin) into the resulting connective tissue pouch and observe the histologic changes characteristic of the three stages of the L-A-S (cf. Figure 2). The first two phases of the local alarm reaction are extremely non-specific: their manifestations are essentially the same, irrespective of the nature of the eliciting injurious agents.[2] There is degeneration and necrosis, followed by edema, with dedifferentiation of sessile mesenchymal elements into polyblasts and infiltration with phagocytes.

However, the original morphologic structure characteristic of the local alarm reaction (like manifestations of the general alarm reaction), cannot

---

[1] H. Selye, 'On the mechanism through which hydrocortisone affects the resistance of tissues to injury.' *J.A.M.A.*, 152:1207, 1953; and 'On the acquisition of tissue resistance to digestion by gastric juice.' *Gastroenterology*. In press.
[2] H. Selye, 'The part of inflammation in the local adaptation syndrome.' in *Symposium on the Mechanism of Inflammation*, eds. G. Jasmin and A. Robert, 1953.

long be maintained. Soon, often within hours, a process of redifferentiation occurs which imparts a certain specificity to the resulting topical tissue-changes. Depending upon the requirements imposed by the irritant used, the dedifferentiated cells are transformed predominantly into fibroblasts, lymphoid elements, macrophages, foreign body giant-cells, etc. Also, depending upon the irritant, varying proportions of hematogenous leukocytes or erythrocytes may accumulate within the injured region. To mention but a few characteristic findings, finely particulate matter stimulates macrophage production, gross particles stimulate giant-cell formation, croton oil stimulates fibroblast proliferation, etc.

It is tempting to assume that the original dedifferentiation of the first stage is a necessary preparation for the second, transformative period, since mature, connective tissue cells are less capable of transformation into entirely different elements than are dedifferentiated, more 'embryonic' cells (e.g., polyblasts).

The striking characteristic of this local stage of resistance is that the wall of the inflammatory focus becomes highly resistant to further treatment with otherwise necrotizing doses of the particular irritant used to produce it (specific resistance). Indeed, it even exhibits a high degree of tolerance to cognate substances which normally would evoke the formation of a histologically similar type of granuloma (crossed resistance). Thus a pouch produced with dilute croton oil becomes resistant to normally necrotizing doses, not only of croton oil itself, but also of formic acid, hypertonic NaCl, mustard oil, NaOH, HCl, trypsin, ox bile and boiling water, and even fresh gastric juice.

Conversely, at this same time, resistance to irritants, which normally would produce different types of granuloma, is significantly diminished (crossed sensitization). Thus a granuloma pouch, formed under the influence of croton oil, undergoes necrosis and perforates readily after injection of formaldehyde or India ink. This is so even if the latter agents are given at dose-levels which would be comparatively well tolerated by the normal (non-irritated) connective tissue surrounding an air-space similar in size and position to that of the granuloma pouch.

Apparently during the local stage of resistance, the wall of an inflammatory focus differentiates in such a manner as to afford optimum protection against the evocative agent or cognate stressors. However, at the same time — and probably as a direct result of this specialized differentiation — it loses the ability to adapt itself for other purposes. Such topical responses are reminiscent of the specific resistance and crossed resistance phenomena which notoriously develop in the organism as a whole, upon exposure to systemic stressors.

Such data suggest a fundamental difference between quantitative and qualitative stress, and indicate the necessity of distinguishing between: homotrophic adaptation, that is, a simple, progressive adaptive phenomenon which can be accomplished without qualitative change by hyperplasia and hypertrophy of pre-existing cell-elements; homoiotropic adaptation, which is called forth whenever a tissue adapted to one function is called upon to perform a slightly different, but cognate activity; and heterotropic adaptation in which a tissue, fully differentiated for one type of action, is forced to readjust to an entirely different activity.

In general the more a cell differentiates for a given function, the less it is capable of heterotropic adaptation. Usually the latter requires more or less complete dedifferentiation to a rather embryonic cell-type, since fully differentiated cell-forms can rarely transform themselves directly into one another. Mitosis is the most effective way of regaining full, juvenile adaptability, by divesting the cell of all its differentiation. Mitotic proliferation is also rarest in highly differentiated cell-types.

Finally, let me call attention to the fact that catabolism, which occurs in both topical and systemic shock, might well be considered a 'chemical dedifferentiation'. The lysis of cellular material liberates chemical substances which can serve as building blocks for the neoformation of tissues adapted to new requirements.

STRESS AND GROWTH

Perhaps the most important feature in this picture is the difficulty of correlating the 'pathologic' phenomena of transformative adaptation (e.g., inflammation) with the 'physiologic' type of simple evolution or progressive tissue-growth. The latter appears to be directed by the laws of heredity, without manifest dependence upon stress.

It is noteworthy that adaptive hormones are important regulators of systemic growth. ACTH and the A-Cs (cortisone, hydrocortisone) are potent growth inhibitors, while STH is so effective in the opposite direction it has actually been called 'the growth hormone'. Systemic stress has a marked inhibitory effect on the growth of the body as a whole, which is mediated, at least in part, through ACTH and the A-Cs.

But is there any link between stress, or adaptive hormones, and the selective topical growth of certain parts which could lead to qualitative changes in morphogenesis? Of course inflammation, one of the salient features of topical stress, is accompanied by pronounced local, proliferative growth phenomena which are often homotropic. Little is known of the possibility of inducing selective growth in certain areas with the aid of topically applied STH, but it is undoubtedly possible to induce a marked selective growth-inhibition by the local application of hydrocortisone to certain predisposed regions.

In many of these instances, topical effects of hormones, upon either inflammation or growth, are manifest only under certain conditions. For example, local vasoconstriction sensitizes to the catabolic (anti-phlogistic) hormones, while local hyperemia enhances the actions of anabolic (prophlogistic) substances such as STH. It has become a major branch of stress research to explore the mechanism through which these conditioning factors alter tissue-reactivity to hormones, but we cannot go into this subject in detail here.

It is also possible that during stress certain cells may develop a special affinity for growth-regulating adaptive hormones, although this is not established with certainty. All these factors could endow certain tissue regions with a selective sensitivity for one or the other type of adaptive hormone, and thus permit the participation of stress in local tissue-growth phenomena.

Perhaps the most important topical stimulant of growth is activity. A muscle cell forced to perform much contractile work, or a glandular cell stimulated to excessive secretory activity, will undergo hypertrophy. Could the stress of local hyperactivity itself act as a conditioning factor for growth-regulating adaptive hormones? Let us re-examine the relationship between stress and specificity.

STRESS AND SPECIFICITY

If stress is defined as a non-specific action-reaction phenomenon, then adaptive tissue-growth, elicited by highly specific stimuli, cannot be so designated. Thus the selective hypertrophy of a muscle caused by frequent stimulation with its specific physiologic excitant, the motor-nerve impulse, is certainly not a stress reaction. It is equally evident, on the other hand, that such specific muscular activity can cause systemic stress, with the accompanying manifestations of a G-A-S. Then what is the relationship between the specific and the non-specific in such responses?

This brings us back to the question of the 'first mediator' of stress reactions. A localized tissue injury, if sufficiently severe, produces not only topical manifestations of the L-A-S, but also mobilizes systemic defence through the G-A-S. Yet we still do not know through which mediators the impulse is carried from the site of the injury to distant parts of the body, for instance, to the pituitary-adrenal axis. The integrity of the innervation in the injured area is not essential since damage to a completely denervated limb can still elicit a G-A-S. Thus humoral stimuli alone appear adequate for the generalization of topical stress-responses, although, of course, nervous stimulation can also act as a systemic stressor.

The humoral transmittor substance(s) in question has been described provisionally as the first mediator(s). Various investigators consider the possibility that locally produced non-specific products of tissue catabolism, polypeptides, histamine, histamine-like compounds, adrenergic or cholinergic substances might be the first mediator. It has been demonstrated that a G-A-S can be produced with any one of these compounds, but all efforts have failed to prove that one of them is the only first mediator of all stress reactions. Indeed, it is even possible the mediation is due not to the presence of humoral substances, but to the absence of some vital blood-constituent which might be avidly used up by damaged tissue, to the detriment of the organism as a whole.

In the genesis of inflammation, mediators have also been postulated. The fact that a stimulus for inflammation could thus be transmitted by humoral means was established. Yet the nature of this phlogistic mediator remains unknown.

The question arises whether the first mediator of the G-A-S (the endogenous stimulus which transmits the stress-message from the injured region to the whole organism and particularly to the pituitary) could be the same as the phlogistic mediator of the L-A-S (the endogenous stimulant of inflammation). Injection of exudate is highly effective in producing a systemic alarm reaction with pronounced ACTH discharge. Could it be that the products of tissue-injury and tissue-activity, if formed in sufficient concentration, are largely responsible both for topical defence phenomena (L-A-S with inflammation) and, if absorbed in sufficient concentration into circulating blood, for alerting the whole organism (eliciting a G-A-S)? In any event, not one of the data now available disproves the possibility of such a close relationship between local and systemic stress responses through the same system of mediation.

To return to a point raised at the end of the preceding section: Is there any relationship between non-specific stress and normal adaptive growth (e.g., of a muscle specifically stimulated by motor impulses)? Let us recall that intense over-exertion of a muscle group can produce a true myositis. Indeed, if such a muscle is subsequently injected with topical irritants, it may reveal a marked local change in local reactivity.[1] This

[1] R. Barany, 'Neurologisch interessante Resultate und Fragestellungen, hervorgegangen aus Untersuchungen ueber aseptische Entzuendung beim Menschen.' *Acta psychiat. et neurol.*, 8:205, 1933.

is just what we would interpret today as a phenomenom of crossed resistance or crossed sensitization. Thus specific stimulation of a target to perform its physiologic work can act as a topical phlogistic (topical stressor) stimulus, at least at certain dose levels. Of course, such specific physiologic stimuli can also cause work hypertrophy. Thereby they predispose the target for the homotropic, adaptive growth-stimulating actions of anabolic hormones, for instance, STH.

The difference between the specific and the non-specific is perhaps more apparent than real. It has been shown that many biologic elements (receptors or targets) can respond to irritation only in one manner. Their reaction-type is conditioned by their own structure, not by the stimulus which activates them, although they may be more sensitive to some stimuli than to others. Whether stimulated by heat, mechanical injury or electricity, a muscle fiber will react with contraction, an optic nerve fiber with the sensation of light, a glandular cell with secretion, and so forth. Could it be that the apparent multiplicity of specific reactions is due merely to combinations and permutations of such single reaction-types of which the various biologic elements of the body are capable? Should this be the case, then all manifestations of life, from the regional to the systemic, from the entirely non-specific to the most highly specific, can be brought down to a common denominator. They would merely represent various groupings of simple, qualitatively unidirectional responses in the diverse biologic units (organs, cells, cell-parts) of the body.

THE FUNCTIONAL UNIT OF LIFE

In 1839 Schleiden and Schwann proposed the 'cell theory' which held that the cell was the fundamental unit of life. Subsequent research has revealed facts incompatible with this theory. Certain slime moulds, for instance, grow to considerable size and yet, though they contain nuclei, show no sign of subdivision into cells. Conversely, erythrocytes contain no nucleus, hence are not true cells. The configuration of viruses is even more remote from the cellular structure, and yet viruses appear to be alive. Finally, there is no valid reason to consider inter-cellular substances as inanimate.

It is illogical that the cell should be the fundamental unit of living organisms since, in a single cell, various portions can perform diverse vital functions simultaneously (e.g., phagocytosis, secretion, perception, locomotion, digestion). Hence an agent can undoubtedly influence one part of the cell (e.g., an organelle) or one biochemical unit (e.g., an enzyme system), selectively. These elementary biologic targets — we might call them 'reactons,' in analogy with other elementary units such as the nephron or neuron — are perhaps also alive. At least, in the absence of evidence to the contrary, we must consider this possibility, since they exhibit the features regarded as characteristic of life, just as much as the entire cell does. Among other things, reactons grow and reproduce their kind. They also have a tendency to maintain their characteristic individuality despite changes in milieu; in other words, they are highly adaptable. Nothing in our observations justifies the conclusion that the essence of these elementary targets is necessarily a somatic structure, that is, matter. It is equally possible the reacton is only a focus of inter-relations, a functional plan or pattern which governs the organization of matter.

The great strength of the cell theory is that one can see the limits of these 'building blocks' and demonstrate that virtually all living matter is made up of them. However, this only shows that the cell is a morphologic unit. But is it the primary unit? Organs are units in the body, tissues are units in the organs, cells are units in the tissues. But must we stop here? The possibility of demonstrating borders by optic means is hardly an adequate reason.

Now the theory of reactons postulates that: (1) The fundamental unit of life has sub-cellular dimensions. This reacton is defined as the smallest target capable of exhibiting biologic reactions. (2) Each reacton can give only one kind of response. The nature of this response depends upon the inherent structure of the reacton itself. Hence at the level of these ultimate units, reaction patterns cannot yet be separated into the specific and non-specific. In other words, the concepts of quality and specificity of response have no meaning here. (3) Specificity of action depends upon the degree of selective affinity which an agent exhibits for certain reactons. (4) Specificity of response depends upon the degree of freedom with which certain reactons can be activated independently of others. (5) Intensity of response depends upon the number of reactons activated. It is still to be determined whether the degree of activation has any importance at this fundamental level, or whether reactons are subject only to the 'triggering' type of yes-or-no response which necessarily leads to the complete discharge of the accumulated action potential. (6) Homotropic adaptation depends upon further work hypertrophy (and/or hyperplasia) of certain previously developed reactons. (7) Heterotropic adaptation depends upon work hypertrophy (and/or hyperplasia) of certain undeveloped reactons, at the expense of inactivity atrophy in others, which were previously developed. This type of response we have been accustomed to regard as a 'qualitative' change. Figure 3 illustrates these thoughts by a simple, mechanical analogy.

(Continued on page 75)

FIGURE 3

In these schematic drawings of the reacton hypothesis, as applied to the interpretation of specific and non-specific actions, reactons are represented by round bodies and interactions between them by straight lines. Although shown here on a single plane, reactons are arranged three-dimensionally in living matter.

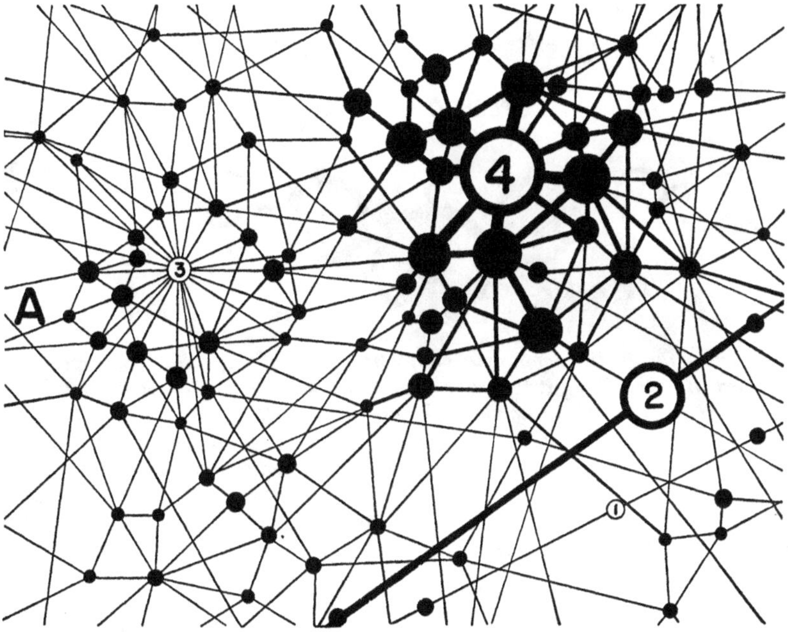

Surface view of field containing reactons in various stages of development and associated by interactions of various importance. One might visualize them as focal knots in a complex network of more or less rigid interactions. Pressure exerted upon any focus will displace others as well, depending upon the number and strength of the connections between the directly affected focus and the rest of the system. The four numbered reactons represent special conditions: (1) undeveloped reacton, directly connected with only two others; (2) developed reacton, directly connected with only two others; (3) undeveloped reacton, directly connected with many others; (4) highly developed reacton, connected with many others. Stimulation at (1) will have a specific effect (2), while stimulation at (3) will have a non-specific effect, even though the agent acted at one point only (4).

Profile view of seven reactons not exposed to any agent. One (3) is most developed while the prominence of the others diminishes as we approach the periphery of the former's activity range. This is a graphic expression of a situation in which (due to genetic factors or previous activity), even at rest, one type of reacton is most developed, while the others have evolved only in proportion to the importance of their interactions with the former (e.g., the reactons directly and more or less indirectly related to contractility in a developed muscle).

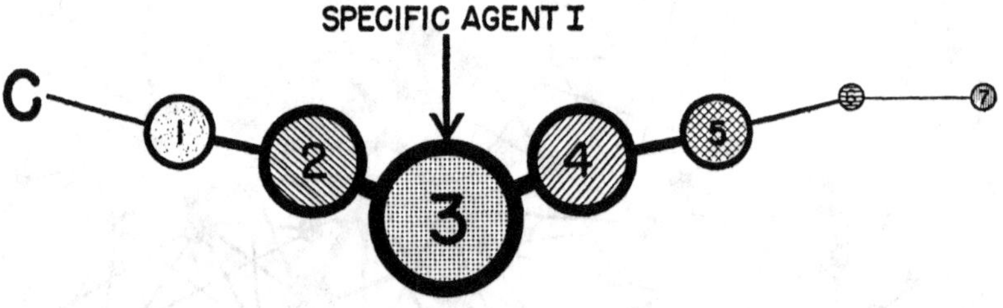

Specific effect with homotropic adaptation. 'Specific agent I' acts upon the system 'B', stimulating it to perform the function for which it has already been specialized. This leads to simple work hypertrophy with a proportionate development of all pertinent reactons and their interactions (e.g., in the above mentioned example of the muscle, the repeated specific stimulation through motor nerve).

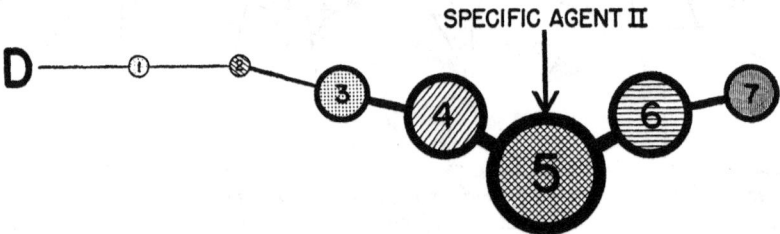

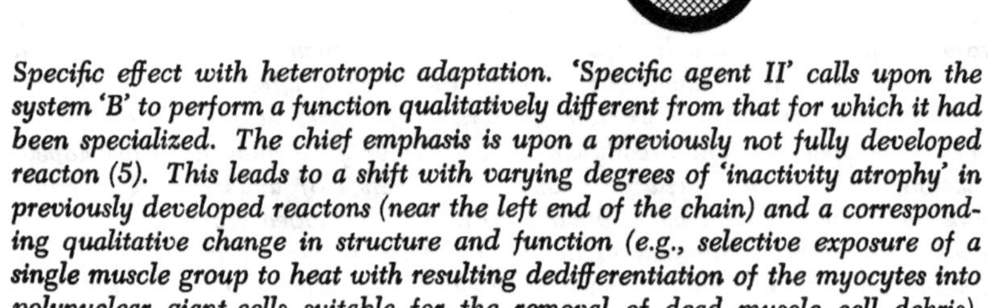

Specific effect with heterotropic adaptation. 'Specific agent II' calls upon the system 'B' to perform a function qualitatively different from that for which it had been specialized. The chief emphasis is upon a previously not fully developed reacton (5). This leads to a shift with varying degrees of 'inactivity atrophy' in previously developed reactons (near the left end of the chain) and a corresponding qualitative change in structure and function (e.g., selective exposure of a single muscle group to heat with resulting dedifferentiation of the myocytes into polynuclear giant-cells suitable for the removal of dead muscle cell debris).

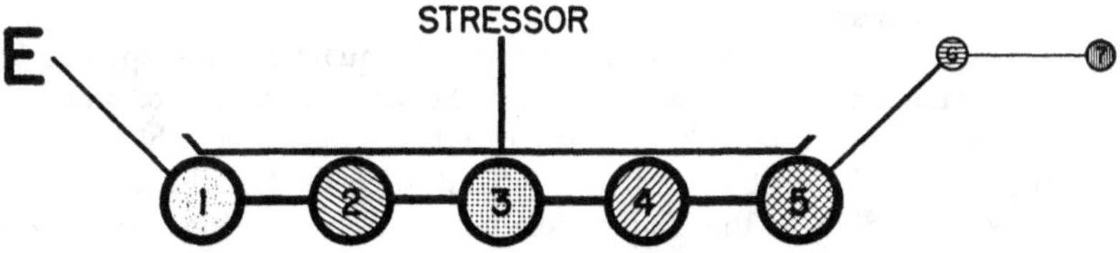

Stress due to non-specific action. Here the nature of the stressor is such that it affects all reactons and their interactions. The corresponding dedifferentiation is illustrated by hypertrophy of the previously underdeveloped (at the expense of involution in the previously most developed) reactons (e.g., exposure of a large tissue area to heat which directly affects all its cells).

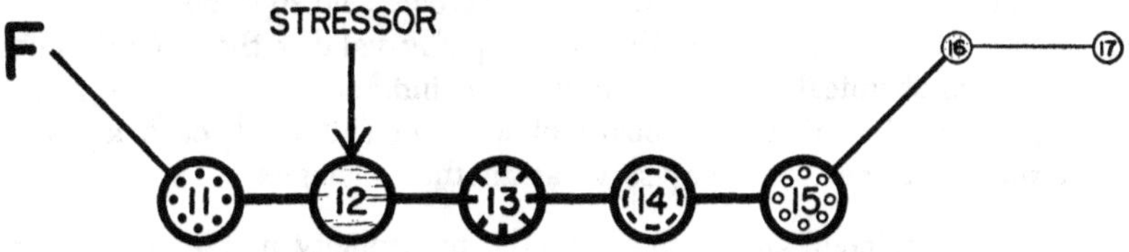

Stress due to non-specific reacton. This also affects all reactons and their bonds in this field, although the stressor acts selectively on (12) alone. The reason for the generalization of the stress effect is the intense dependence of (11-15) upon each other in this particular field. Thus the response of (12) immediately produces marked repercussions in all others within the system (e.g., overstimulation of the adrenal nerves, whose direct effect is highly specific, but the resulting adrenaline-discharge produces a widespread stress response).

(Continued from page 71)

It may be difficult to comprehend how simple quantitative responses in a limited number of reactons might give the virtually unlimited number of apparently quantitatively distinct reaction-patterns of which living matter is capable. Yet this is not without precedent in biology. For instance, according to the Young-Helmholtz theory of vision, there are only three fundamental colour sensations: red, green and violet. By suitable combinations, all other colours can be formed. To explain this, it was assumed that there existed three kinds of nerve elements in the retina, each of which was specifically responsive to the stimulus waves of a certain frequency, corresponding to one colour. If the nerve elements corresponding to red and green were simultaneously set in action, the resulting sensation would be orange or yellow; if green and violet, the sensation would be blue or indigo, etc. Actually, no such nerve fibers or elements are known, but the theory is equally valid if the stimuli affect three photo-chemical substance units. The innumerable melodies which can be derived from the keyboard of a piano (although each key can reproduce but one tone) may serve as another analogy.

It is not too difficult to imagine that the multiplicity in the patterns of reaction, of which any cell is capable, could thus be synthetized by simple yes-or-no responses of its constituent reactons. In all these instances, the quality of the true fundamental unit (as the pure colour, the pure tone) is invariable. Differences in kind cannot occur at the level of elements, but the impression of a qualitative change is created by mixtures of immutable fundamental units.

SUMMARY

Let us recapitulate. We defined stress as a non-specific adaptive syndrome. By studying the chronologic evolution of systemic stress, we arrived at the concept of the general adaptation syndrome. An enquiry into the effect of stress applied to circumscribed tissue regions revealed the existence of a closely related, but topographically more limited local adaptation syndrome. This led us to explore the behaviour of individual cells under stress where it became evident that, while undergoing adaptation, even a single cell could respond with many qualitatively different biologic reaction forms, both specific and non-specific.

All these studies highlighted the difference between homotropic adaptation (simple quantitative progression along phylogenetically and ontogenetically established lines) and heterotropic adaptation (dedifferentiation to secure building blocks for subsequent qualitative reconstruction). Since even a single cell proved capable of heterotropic adaptation by re-arrangement of biologic elements, it could not in itself be regarded as the fundamental unit of living matter. This led to the hypothesis of the reactons, which postulated that sub-cellular units could exhibit the generally accepted characteristics of life.

There is no evidence that new reactons can be created from any source other than preformed reactons of the same kind. The old adage *Omnis cellula e cellula ejusdem generis* really does not hold true for the cell (e.g., metaplasia, neoplasia); perhaps it would be more accurate to say, *Omne reacton e reactone ejusdem generis.*

In the light of this hypothesis, some basic concepts in biology may be formulated as follows: growth is multiplication or enlargement of reactons; specificity is selective responsiveness of certain kinds of reactons; homotropic adaptation is further activation and growth of previously developed reactons; heterotropic adaptation is activation and growth of dormant reactons, with relative regression of those which previously were most prominent.

As I see it, the basic task is now to find objective means to test the validity of the principal deduction, namely, that all vital phenomena depend merely upon quantitative variations in the activation of preexistent elementary targets.

Hans Selye

ART AND SCIENCE

No sooner do I form a conception of a material or corporeal substance, than I feel the need of conceiving that it has boundaries and shape; that relative to others it is great or small; that it is in this place or that; that it is moving or still; that it touches or does not touch another body; that it is unique, rare or common; nor can I, by any effort of imagination, disjoin it from these qualities. On the other hand, I find no need to apprehend it as accompanied by such conditions as whiteness or redness, bitterness or sweetness, sonorousness or silence, well-smelling or ill-smelling. If the senses had not informed us of these qualities, language and imagination alone could never have arrived at them. Wherefore I hold that tastes, colors, smells and the like exist only in the being which feels, which being removed, these qualities themselves do vanish. Having special names for them we would persuade ourselves that these have a real and veritable existence. But I hold that there exists nothing in external bodies for exciting tastes, smells and sounds but size, shape, quantity and motion. If, therefore, the organs of sense, ears, tongues and noses were removed, I believe that shape, quantity and motion would remain, but there would be no more of smells, tastes and sounds. Thus, apart from the living creatures, I take these to be mere words.

Galileo Galilei
Il Saggiatore, 1624

Here are the beginnings of the widely held belief that art and science are polar opposites, mutually exclusive in their aims, methods and results. The view that quantitative, measurable attributes of things are real and that direct sensory experience is unreal and untrustworthy leads quite logically to a value judgment favorable to science and unfavorable to art. The one becomes approved for its rationality and precision, the other distrusted as subjective, untestable and prelogical. The distinction which Galileo drew was an intellectual necessity for the development of the exact sciences. But the separation between art and science in our minds is no longer useful and will not bear close scrutiny.

History shows us that these two creative human activities are interdependent, no matter which of the two the times emphasize more strongly. Each achieves stronger growth when cross-pollinated by the other. Indeed, the rebirth of that interest in scientific knowledge which has led to the great scientific discoveries of the past five centuries was primarily an achievement of great painters, sculptors and architects of the Renaissance. The work of such men as Masaccio, Alberti, Pollaiuolo, Leonardo and Durer was as much systematic inquiry into the structure of the natural world as it was imaginative creation of visual forms to move the spectator. Their concrete and communicable vision of natural order proved as fateful for the development of science as for the development of art; it can be called art or science with equal validity. At certain times in history, more attention was focused on art than on science; today those relative positions are reversed. At no time, however, has one existed independently of the other. In our age of specialization the artist and the scientist are almost never the same person — a circumstance which obscures but does not alter the connection between art and science.

Art and science are ordering activities of the human mind. Through sifting and organizing the order relations impressed on us by our senses, they distill our significant experience and bring us insight into the order relations of nature.

Science attempts to discern order relations in nature, making verifiable statements about the external world. Data are set out in terms of measured quantities; and the found order is expressed in terms of conceptual structures.

Art attempts to discern order relations in nature, creating images of our experience of the world. Data are set out in terms of recreated sensed forms; and the felt order is expressed in terms of sensible structures exhibiting properties of harmony, rhythm and proportion.

Images are the elemental stuff of all our thinking and feeling. Of a feeling of warmth, the smell of milk, the touch of hands, the looming of features, the child compounds a unified picture of the mother. Image making — the integration of sense data into a coherent experience of something — is thinking and feeling on the most elementary level. Through images we participate in the world, responding emotionally to its sensible qualities and rhythms. We mobilize ourselves to recreate its felt patterns. 'Mommy,' the child says. Through images we become aware of the world's forms and structures. We mobilize ourselves to develop ideas and concepts. 'Mommies,' the child says later on, filling out a model of adult femininity.

Image making is basic for art. It is basic for science, too, defining goals, delimiting fields for study and providing sense models which anticipate the corresponding scientific statements of order relations. On the image-making level, the difference between pre-scientific and pre-artistic perception of order is a difference of attitude, an attention to structure, on the one hand, or to the felt quality of experience, on the other. There is no particular need for these attitudes to be mutually exclusive. Structures can be grasped and qualities can be felt in a single, balanced perception of order, in an experience which has characteristics of scientific and artistic activity both. This balance is also possible on complex levels; one and the same set of created symbols can evoke an intense emotional response to the richness of its sensed patterns and convey an idea of logical structure.

Some men, at nearly all times, have produced work which combines profoundly moving patterns of sense with a profound perception of mathematical order. Bach, in music, Poussin, in painting, present us with exquisitely patterned sense models of an orderly world.

Brief periods in history, both in Western Europe and in the Asiatic East, reached a kind of cultural equilibrium, a common life of the emotions and the intellect. In Renaissance Italy, in Sung China, men were gripped by the emotional excitement of rediscovery of the world as they tried to make the world's order intelligible and clear. In single, fused statements of natural order they recorded nature's structural articulation and expressed its harmonies and moods. With a Sung landscape painting or a fresco by Piero della Francesca, we enter a society in which scientific and artistic attitudes dwelt together, not apart.

But, East and West, the trend of centuries has brought imbalance of intellect and feeling. The East has moved in one direction, the West in the other. The anatomy of the world preoccupies us in the West; our culture centres upon objective understanding of substance, forces and structures, to the impoverishment of our subjective appreciation of patterns and rhythms. The East has concerned itself not with the world's structure but with its physiognomy, and has institutionalized, as the West has not, highly developed appreciation of its harmonies, its tastes and flavours.

Today, with all lands knit together by new tools of communication and world-embracing political forms, it has become possible to exchange attitudes as well as ideas. A pooling of Western structural discipline and Oriental emotional discipline could contribute to cultural equilibrium – on a higher level, this time, with a heightening of our ability to understand the world and read its significance.

The Far Eastern discipline of sensibilities grew out of the feeling that men lived most fully by opening themselves to the universal rhythm of Nature. Nature was approached and entered through rapt contemplation of its forms, to the end of visualizing the world in terms not of likeness but of what the Chinese called 'rhythmical vitality' – the essence of things in their characteristic life of movement. The patterns seen were not frameworks binding details but patterns of living order. The story is told that Rykku, the Japanese master of the tea ceremony, instructed his son to clean the garden before the arrival of guests. Inspecting the immaculately finished result, he said to the youth, 'This is not the way,' and shook a tree so that leaves fell in a free pattern across a path. Thus, the man-made structural order of the garden was united with the natural order of living forms.

At times, Western poets and thinkers have given us a vision of this accord between man and nature. 'The greatest good,' said Spinoza, 'is the knowledge of the union which the mind has with the whole of nature.' Thoreau said, 'Some time, as I drift idly along Walden Pond, I cease to live and begin to be.'

In the West, the visualization of our experience has been looked at as the fashioning of representations of nature, likenesses of the things around us. This is the Aristotelian tradition; and, particularly since the Renaissance, it has been assumed that fidelity to the optical appearance of objects is the only means of artistic description of reality. Nevertheless, at all times master works of art have transcended mere representation; and during the past seventy-five years Western art has shifted toward ideas and methods corresponding to this Far Eastern vision. What the artist Piet Mondrian lately called the 'liberated and universal rhythm distorted and hidden in the individual rhythm of limiting forms', the great pioneers of modern art have tried to make visible. Today artists more often depict the inner world of man than the likeness of particular objects, making visible and external their experience of connection with the world around them. But the general public, most scientists included, still assumes that art is naturalistic representation.

The essential vision of reality presents us not with fugitive appearances but with felt patterns of order which have coherence and meaning for the eye and for the mind. Harmony, balanced and rhythmic sequence express essential characteristics of natural phenomena: the connectedness of nature — the order, the logic, the living process. Here art and science can meet on common ground.

Most scientists feel that conceptual thinking has transcended the power of visualization to aid them in describing the new worlds of science. Immersed in the tradition that visualization is static representation of objects, they could hardly have escaped entertaining this view. Recognition that visualization is much more than this, can bring to them a stimulus to their thinking that they now deny themselves. Artistic expression comes to conclusions similar to those of science, finding idioms for the description of processes and relations. Here is reinforcement for science, an increase of power, a source of breadth to counterbalance the limitations which science systematically sets for itself.

Contemporary scientists recognize that visual models of their new concepts cannot be provided by a portrayal of things; it is a model of relatedness that is called for. Artistic expressions which convey a sense of relatedness can provide science with new resources for visualization. In a closer communion between artists and scientists it may be possible to work out new visual idioms to reinforce the abstract concept by the powerful, immediate sensory image which conveys the same meaning.

The psychology of sense perception has taught us that without the use of both eyes, without a binocular vision, there would be no awareness of the third dimension of space. The depth of human experience in the same sense depends on the fact that we are able to vary our modes of seeing, that we can alternate our views of reality. *Rerum videre formas* is no less important and indispensable task than *rerum cognoscere causas.*

Ernst Cassirer
An Essay on Man

Scientists are aware of the role of what they call 'intuition' in the creative process whereby they integrate their data into new expressions of order. They are often aware also of the closeness of their creative thoughts to visual and artistic thinking — they 'look forward' to certain types of results;

they 'design' their experiments and their apparatus. Their procedure in presenting results, however, gives us no hint of this. We are shown logical steps by which knowledge can be verified; we are not shown the deep workings of human minds.

The scientist anticipates his results, above all to the extent of addressing himself to his problem by visualizing it. His results take shape in part as a set of connected images, grasped, understood, attached to previous experience. This is not to say that his investigation will not overrun the boundaries of the visualized goals — science is often a runaway process. Often expressions are arrived at, the use and significance of which are unclear. A basic mathematical concept is the square root of minus one — De Moivre's *i*. *i* was unanticipated, emerging from mathematical manipulation. It was called 'imaginary' as opposed to the other 'real' numbers with which men had been familiar; it disturbed mathematicians by presenting a breach in their orderly structure of concepts. Its menace departed, however, when expressions containing *i* found simple geometrical demonstrations and practical uses gave *i* a meaningful place in the real world.

Mathematicians who build new spaces and physicists who find them in the universe can profit from study of the pictorial and architectural spaces conceived and built by men of art. The finite universe of late medieval times found a pictorial counterpart in the limited, shallow, 'abstract' spaces of Giotto. Stage by stage, art kept pace with developing cosmological concepts until, in the Italian Renaissance, the artists became the cosmologists themselves. Of all artists, the Greeks alone reveal space conceptions limited by Euclidian geometry. The past seven centuries have given us the 'symbolic' space of the early Flemish masters; the 'rational' space of fifteenth century Renaissance Italy, deep and clear; the 'ideal' space of Raphael and the High Renaissance, in which a clear foreground, continuing the spatial characteristics of the world in which the observer finds himself, converges upon a spatially mysterious, otherworldly realm; the soaring, levitational space of Gothic cathedrals; the poised and balanced spatial volumes of the High Renaissance church of San Biagio at Montepulciano; the 'exploding' space of the German Baroque at Vierzehnheiligen; the pervasive space of the Impressionists, dissolving all solid form; the laminated, timebound space of the later Cubists.

At present, our powers of abstract analysis seem to have outstripped our powers of visualization — hence the doubt that new theories can be visualized. Some of these doubts are unfounded; for example, it is doubted that a sense model can be found of a four-dimensional continuum, of space-time. An art form of the baroque era — the opera — prefigured scientific expression of four-dimensionality, suggesting continuous transformation by combining pictorial forms with temporal sequences of melody and rhythm in music, acting and dancing. And the stroboscopic action sequence brings us close to a model of the space-time motion of contemporary physical theories when it shows us successive stages of a form generating a virtual volume, mapping a four-dimensional phenomenon upon a two-dimensional area. There is no need that pictorial models of new relationships be maintained within the limits of Euclidean geometry — far from it. The new events of science have been complemented by a new range of sensibility with which to sense the newly discovered complex worlds.

Science expands the area of generalization; discrete terrains are linked in common formulations. The larger the areas that are brought into the same scale and meaning, the more important becomes awareness of form relationships; we focus less and less on the facts themselves and more and more upon their interconnection. Thus, in its evolution, science approaches art.

We have accumulated so vast and complex a store of scientific knowledge today that we need a new kind of science to describe the essential motifs of the whole in a unity.

It is becoming apparent that the metrical aspects alone of all subjects cannot express all of the things in which scientists, as such, are interested, and the development of the mathematical theory of relationships other than metrical will be a great help to scientific research when it has to face either problems of greater complexity in inorganic nature, or any problems in organic nature. In the most recent work in physics as in wave mechanics or in biological problems (including the unsolved problems of civilization) both the whole and the parts must be continually kept in mind. The metre rule is no longer the physicist's magic wand, alone capable of dealing with all problems of physics, and outside the laboratory the ourselves-alone idea of, for example, intense nationalism, in practice does not work. Both inside the laboratory and outside, man is meeting problems needing "contrapuntal' thinking, or, to vary the metaphor, needing the type of mental activity usually associated with the artist who can pay infinite attention to detail without losing sight of the whole.

William H. George
The Scientist in Action

Art can make an important contribution by providing insights into structural correspondence common to the various disciplines of science but ignored because science, of necessity, isolates and limits its fields and objectives.

Gyorgy Kepes

A TYPOLOGY OF FUNCTIONAL ANALYSIS

The term 'functionalism' has been a favourite concept in the social sciences for almost twenty-five years. Indeed, it would be no exaggeration to say that far from being a neutral concept, 'functionalism' has become an honorific term surrounded by an intense 'halo effect'.[1] Most researchers are not content to stop with a 'structural' analysis of their data, but feel constrained at least to point out their 'functional' implications. Despite the plethora of functional analyses, however, 'functionalism' has remained a vague and sometimes confusing concept.

The first confusion inherent in the use of 'functionalism' arises from a failure to distinguish between functionalism as a *philosophy* of culture and functionalism as a *method* of studying and analyzing culture. Functionalism as philosophy has tended to be dogmatic, as any theory which is not controlled by empirical data tends to become dogmatic. It asserts, as an axiom to be accepted rather than as a hypothesis to be tested, that all aspects of culture are functional (for the moment, the term will remain undefined). Malinowski, for example, writes: 'The functional view of culture insists therefore upon the principle that in every type of civiliza-

---

1 But see Dorothy Gregg and Elgin Williams, 'The Dismal Science of Functionalism.' *American Anthropologist*, 50:594-611, 1948.

tion, every custom, material object, idea and belief fulfills some vital function. . .'.[1]

Functionalism, as method, makes no *a priori* assertions about culture; it attempts, rather, to discover empirically what functional relationships, if any, do exist. But the problem of ambiguity still remains; for different authors often mean quite different things by the same term, and the same author may at times use the term in quite different ways. The concern of this paper is with functionalism as method. Its purpose is not to indicate which use of the term is the correct or proper one, but to distinguish the various ways in which it has been used – with the thought that confusion can be avoided if these different usages are explicitly distinguished.

An analysis of the ways in which methodological functionalism has been used yields, with some difficulty, a three-fold classification which we shall label teleologic, genetic, and configurational. Each of these categories can be subdivided so as to give us six meanings of the term as currently employed; some of these in turn may be further divided into 'latent' and 'manifest' functions, to employ terms suggested by Merton.[2] The rest of this paper will be devoted to an analysis of this classification, outlined below:

	TELEOLOGIC		GENETIC		CONFIGURATIONAL	
	Socio-logical	Psycho-biological	Phylo-genetic	Onto-genetic	Social	Psychological
Manifest						
Latent						

'Teleologic functionalism' is used here to designate that position which identifies the function of a cultural institution with its consequences. This type of functionalism can be subdivided into 'sociological' and 'psychobiological' functionalism. By 'sociological functionalism' we shall designate that position which sees as the end or consequence of an institution the contribution it makes to the survival or welfare of the society. Thus, Radcliffe-Brown writes: 'I would define the social function of a socially standardized mode of activity, or mode of thought, as its relation to the social structure, to the existence and continuity of which it makes some contribution.'[3] Linton expresses a similar notion when he writes that 'the function of a trait-complex is the sum total of its contribution

---

[1] B. Malinowski, 'Anthropology.' *Encyclopedia Britannica*, 1926, p. 32.
[2] Robert Merton, *Social Theory and Social Structure*, 1949, ch. 1.
[3] A. R. Radcliffe-Brown, 'On Social Structure.' *Journal of the Royal Anthropological Institute*, 70:9-10, 1940.

towards the perpetuation of the social-cultural configuration.'[1] Durkheim's study of Australian totemism[2] and Radcliffe-Brown's analysis of Andamanese ceremonial life[3] are excellent examples of this type of functional analysis.

By 'psychobiological functionalism' we mean to designate the position which seeks the consequence of an institution in the contribution it makes to the biological or psychological welfare of the individual. Malinowski, for example, writes that 'culture appears first and foremost as a vast instrumental reality . . . which allow(s) man to satisfy his biological requirements through cooperation. . .'.[4] Examples of studies employing psychobiological functionalism are to be found in Hallowell's analysis of Ojibwa sorcery[5] and Kluckhohn's interpretation of Navaho witchcraft.[6]

This classification is not meant to imply that any given author does not employ both kinds of teleologic functionalism. Indeed, cultural research often demands both kinds of analysis. Kluckhohn and Nadel, for example, use both types and clearly distinguish between them. 'A given bit of culture', writes Kluckhohn, 'is "functional" insofar as it defines a mode of response which is adaptive from the standpoint of the society and adjustive from the standpoint of the individual.'[7] Nadel expresses the same point when he writes: 'We have, then, two sets of "functions"—the fulfillment of the necessities of group existence, and the fulfillment of biological and psycho-physical necessities.'[8]

'Genetic functionalism' is not concerned with the consequences of an institution, nor is it concerned with the relationship between an institution and an individual. Its concern is with the relationship that obtains between an institution and one or more other institutions, such that the existence of the one is a necessary condition for the other, or such that a change in one leads to a change in the other. As Chapple and Coon put it: '"Functional dependence" is exhibited when there is such a relationship between phenomena that a value of one variable changes uniformly with changes in another (x varies as a function of y).'[9]

---

1 Ralph Linton, *The Study of Man*, 1936, p. 404.
2 Emile Durkheim, *The Elementary Forms of Religious Life*, 1915.
3 A. R. Radcliffe-Brown, *The Andaman Islanders*, 1933, ch. 5.
4 B. Malinowski, 'The Group and the Individual in Functional Analysis.' *American Journal of Sociology*, 44, 1939, p. 962. This also seems to be the thesis of his posthumous volume, *A Scientific Theory of Culture*, 1944. In other places, for example 1926 *op cit.*, he is a sociological functionalist. In his 1939 paper, *op cit.*, p. 946, he is both a sociological and psychological functionalist. And in his published fieldwork, for example *Argonauts of the Western Pacific*, 1922, he is a configurational functionalist.
5 A. Irving Hallowell, 'Aggression in Saulteux Society.' *American Anthropologist*, 42:395-407, 1940.
6 Clyde Kluckhohn, 'Navaho Witchcraft.' *Papers of the Peabody Museum*, 22:2, 1944.
7 Kluckhohn, *op cit.*, p. 47.
8 S. F. Nadel, *The Foundations of Social Anthropology*, 1951, p. 373.
9 Eliot Dismore Chapple and Carleton Stevens Coon, *Principles of Anthropology*, 1942, p. 4; also A. Lesser, 'Functionalism in Social Anthropology.' *American Anthropologist*, 37:386-393, 1935.

Like teleologic functionalism, genetic functionalism, too, may be divided into two sub-types: phylogenetic and ontogenetic. 'Phylogenetic functionalism' is concerned with the relationship between two elements of culture which originated in different periods of the history of a society, such that one can be said to have been a condition for the emergence of the other (this relationship is functional rather than causal for reasons to be pointed out below). Such is the relationship between Calvinism and modern capitalism as analyzed by Weber[1] or between acculturation and nativistic movements.[2]

'Ontogenetic functionalism', on the other hand, is concerned with institutions which co-exist in the same cultural time unit – and which are thus learned by each generation – in which one is viewed as a condition for the existence of the other. Examples of such studies are, Nadel's analysis of the relationship between Mesakin kinship and witchcraft[3] and Kardiner's analysis of the Marquesan pattern of male-female interaction and belief in familiar spirits.[4]

Upon reflection, it is evident that functional genetic relationships are indirect rather than direct, in that the dependent cultural variable is related to the independent cultural variable by means of an intervening psychological variable.[5] Calvinism, acculturation, a particular kind of kinship, and a unique form of sexual interaction, as independent variables, are neither necessary nor sufficient conditions for the existence of capitalism, nativistic movements, witchcraft, and familiar spirits, respectively. (If they were, the relationship would be causal.) But these independent cultural variables are sufficient conditions for the emergence of *attitudes* toward work, status *insecurity*, old-age *anxiety*, and sexual *fears*, respectively. And these intervening psychological variables (attitudes, anxiety, etc.) may be seen to be the necessary, but not sufficient, conditions for the existence of the dependent cultural variables listed above. In short, in all cases of genetic functionalism, with the exception of changes induced by technology or by the physical environment, the dependent institution is related to the independent institution as an expression or satisfaction of the psychological needs or drives created by the latter.[6] The quali-

---

1 Max Weber, *The Protestant Ethic and the Spirit of Capitalism*, 1930.

2 Ralph Linton, 'Nativistic Movements.' *American Anthropologist*, 45:230-240, 1943.

3 S. F. Nadel, 'Witchcraft in Four African Societies: An Essay in Comparison.' *American Anthropologist*, 54:18-29, 1952.

4 Abram Kardiner, *The Individual and His Society*, 1939, ch. 6.

5 Three very useful analyses of the concept of 'intervening variable' and of the role it plays in scientific analysis may be found in: K. MacCorquodale and P. E. Meehl, 'On a Distinction between Hypothetical Constructs and Intervening Variables.' *Psychological Review*, 55:95-107, 1948; Theodore M. Newcomb, *Social Psychology*, 1950, ch. 1; and Edward Chace Tolman, 'Physiology, Psychology, and Sociology.' *Psychological Review*, 45:228-241, 1938.

6 If this analysis is correct we may see the pitfalls inherent in that position which insists that socio-cultural behaviour must be explained on its own 'level', and that the introduction of psychological constructs as explanatory concepts involves a false reductionism.

fication in this generalization is important because technological or environmental changes may compel institutional changes regardless of any psychological condition. The destruction of the buffalo, for example, compelled the Plains Indians to seek another source of livelihood.

If this analysis is correct, it is apparent why the above studies are studies of functional, rather than of causal, relationships. It is impossible to establish a lawful statement to the effect that Calvinism causes capitalism; antagonism between mother's brother and sister's son causes witchcraft; acculturation causes nativistic movements; etc. Instead we find that these institutions or conditions give rise to certain psychological needs, drives, or sets. Now if these intervening psychological variables had predictable consequences, we could still establish causal connections. But this is not the case, for a number of institutions may satisfy the need or reduce the drive or express the feeling aroused by the prior institution. Thus, the psychological variable is, as it were, a genotypic stimulus which may give rise to a number of phenotypically different responses. This fact is expressed by the concept of 'functional equivalence', which states that 'just as the same item may have multiple functions, so may the same function be diversely fulfilled by alternative items. Functional needs are . . . taken to be permissive, rather than determinant of specific social structures.'[1]

It must be noted, however, that though the same psychological response may give rise to a number of diverse institutions, the relationship between the institution and this response is not fortuitous. For however different these institutions may be in *form* and in *content*, they all serve the same function: namely, to satisfy, reduce, or express the psychological state.

Failure to recognize this last point has given rise to many theoretical controversies — such as the controversy over the importance of childhood experiences. Some of the more extreme proponents of the importance of childhood experiences may have given the impression that a particular socialization technique 'causes' a particular adult institution. Their critics have pointed out that two societies may have similar socialization techniques and yet have different adult institutions, or different socialization techniques, and the same adult institutions. Hence they conclude that adult culture has little, if any, connection with childhood experiences. But genetic-functional analysis reveals that neither position is valid. Institutions cannot cause institutions; they only cause psychological states (needs, drives, etc.). But since different socialization practices may give rise to the same psychological state (insecurity, for example, may be evoked by many diverse stimuli), and since this psychological state may

---

[1] Merton, *op cit.*, p. 25; also H. G. Barnett, 'Cultural Processes.' *American Anthropologist*, 42:21-48, 1940.

seek different types of expression (insecurity may be reduced by art, religion, psychotherapy, etc.), it is impossible to predict that given childhood experiences and adult institutions are therefore not related is a *non sequitir*, for though they are not causally related, they may well be functionally related.

In a genetic functional analysis of this problem we are confronted with two institutions and a psychological state – in which the psychological state, as the intervening variable, serves as the dependent variable with respect to one institution, and as the independent variable with respect to the other institution. Thus, a given socialization practice(s), viewed as the independent variable, x, evokes a psychological response in the child – let us say, insecurity – which is the dependent variable, y. The paradigm below indicates that x is a sufficient, but not a necessary, condition for y,

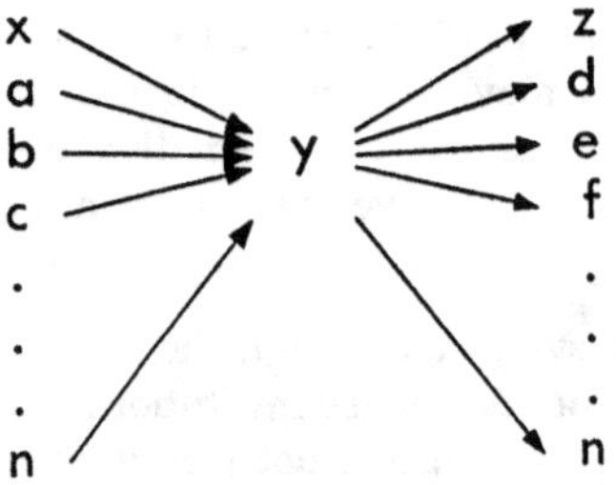

since a,b,c,...n could also have evoked y. (Insecurity, for example, could be evoked by beating, castration threats, threats of supernatural punishment, a highly competitive school system, etc.).

Now if we assume that psychological states are dynamic forces which seek expression within the environment, and not merely static events that remain encapsulated within the organism, we are then justified in further assuming that this psychological state will have some behavioural manifestation. And since this psychological state is shared (since most, if not all, members of the society experience the same socialization practices), it is highly probable that the behavioural manifestation will also be shared, that is, institutionalized. The psychological state, y, is now taken as the independent variable which we wish to relate to some institution, z, taken as the dependent variable. But just as different childhood practices may give rise to the same psychological state, so different institutions may express this state, as the paradigm indicates. (Insecurity may be expressed in religion, art, folklore, etc.). Hence y is a necessary but not a sufficient, condition for z; for if y were not present, z would not be present. But the form taken by z is dependent not only upon y, but upon a host of other psychological, cultural, and historical factors.

'Configurational functionalism' is concerned neither with the social or individual ends served by an institution, nor with the relationship between any two institutions, but, rather, with the interdependence of all the institutions of a culture. As Herskovits has put it:

> The functional view attempts to study the interrelations between the various elements, small and large, in a culture. Its object is essentially to achieve some expression of the unities of culture by indicating how trait and complex and pattern, however separable they may be, intermesh, as the gears of some machine to constitute a smoothly running, affectively functioning whole.[1]

Like the other categories, 'configurational functionalism', too, may be subdivided, into what may be called 'social' and 'psychological' functionalism. 'Social functionalism' is concerned with the analysis of social integration, that is, with the extent to which the various elements of culture are consistent with each other and do not conflict. Malinowski's study of the kula[2] remains the classic example of this kind of functionalism.

'Psychological functionalism' is not so much concerned with the relations among the various elements of culture as in the relation between these elements and some higher order concept which serves to integrate them by infusing them with common psychological meaning. This concept is usually termed the *ethos* of a culture. Benedict's *Patterns of Culture* remains the classic example of this category, but there have been a number of other studies of 'ethos' since.[3]

We have been able, then, to distinguish six meanings of 'functionalism'. But this classification is not finished. Not only may the term 'functionalism' refer to one of these six categories, but each of these categories, in turn, may present the culture or institution as it is perceived by the scientist or as it is perceived by the actors, the members of the society. That is, it is possible that functional relationships are relationships of which the people themselves are aware, or which they have contrived; or that these relationships are discovered by the scientist, though the people themselves are unaware of them. Merton has suggested — following Freud —

---

1 M. J. Herskovits, *Man and His Works*, 1948, p. 215.

2 Malinowski, 1922, *op cit.*

3 Cf., Gregory Bateson, *Naven*, 1936; J. J. Honigmann, 'Culture and Ethos in Kaska Society.' *Yale University Publications in Anthropology*, 40, 1949; E. G. Burrows, 'From Value to Ethos on Ifaluk Atoll.' *Southwestern Journal of Anthropology*, 8:13-35, 1952.

the terms 'manifest' and 'latent' to distinguish these two levels of analysis. 'Manifest function' refers to these functions '. . . which are intended and recognized by particular participants in the system', whereas 'latent functions' are '. . . those which are neither intended nor recognized.'[1]

This distinction between 'manifest' and 'latent' function is extremely important, for as students of culture, we are at least as interested in the meaning of behaviour, as we are in the behaviour itself. It is crucial to know, therefore, whether the 'meaning' (that is, function) which an anthropologist ascribes to an institution is one the people themselves ascribe to their behaviour, in which case it has one significance; or whether it is a meaning which the analysis of the anthropologist has discovered, but of which the people are unaware, in which case it has quite a different significance. The failure to draw this distinction has resulted in much futile controversy over such questions as the nature and function of religion, of avoidance taboos, of the family, and of many others.

Thus far this paper has indicated that the term 'functionalism' has been used in a number of different ways, which can be classified into three bifurcated classes, which in turn may be cut across by a dichotomous class. It is apparent that we seriously abuse the English language and, what is worse, obfuscate some important theoretical and methodological issues unless we indicate which use we are employing in any given context. This may be illustrated with an example from the author's research.

In one of the author's original drafts of a chapter on Ifaluk religion, he wrote that unlike western religion, Ifaluk religion is 'functional', and, again, in describing the Ifaluk belief in malevolent ghosts *(alus)*, he wrote that it was 'functional'.[2] It is now apparent that these statements are hopelessly ambiguous, and require important qualifications if they are to convey any information about Ifaluk religion; for in the light of the typology presented in this paper this statement could refer to one, some, or all of the twelve current 'usages' of 'functionalism'. Hence, the reader would either remain in ignorance, or he would interpret the sentence in terms of his own usage of 'function', in which case he might entirely misinterpret the statement.

In the light of what we know about Ifaluk culture, and in terms of the

---

[1] Merton, *op cit.*, p. 51. Merton restricts the use of 'function' to the category which we have termed 'teleologic'; and it may well be that for purposes of clarity it would be most efficient to adopt this restricted use, and use other terms to designate the other categories. Our concern in this paper, however, has been to indicate and classify the diverse ways in which the term has been used, rather than to indicate how it ought to be used.

[2] A description of Ifaluk culture can be found in E. G. Burrows and M. E. Spiro, *An Atoll Culture: Ethnography of Little Disturbed Ifaluk in the Central Carolines.* Human Relations Area Files, New Haven, 1953.

typology presented in this paper, the Ifaluk belief in malevolent ghosts may be shown to have the following 'functions'.[1]

1 It provides both the group and the individual with an explanation for illness and for anti-social behaviour. (Manifest teleologic functionalism — both biopsychological and sociological.)

2 The people account for the existence of these ghosts by saying that they are the souls of those dead Ifaluk who were evil while they were alive. (Manifest genetic functionalism — ontogenetic.)

3 It is integrated with other religious beliefs, such as the belief in the identical immortal existence for every person — since an evil person is not responsible for his activity, he is not to be punished for it. It is integrated with medicine — public prophylactic and therapeutic ceremonies involving defence against, and exorcism of, the ghosts. It is integrated with technology — rituals performed in the construction of canoes or buildings to prevent destruction by ghosts. It is integrated with infant and child care — customs to prevent the ghosts from attacking children by covering their faces with a cloth so that the ghosts do not recognize them, or obstructing the doorway with mats so that they should not be able to enter. (Manifest configurational functionalism — social.)

4 It is integrated with their ethos of non-aggression by their refusal to punish or chastise a hostile person, diagnosed as *malebush* (possessed by a malevolent ghost), since he is deemed not responsible for his behaviour. (Manifest configurational functionalism — Psychological.)

5 It preserves the solidarity of the group by permitting the people to displace their aggression into ghosts, rather than direct them against their own fellows. (Latent teleologic functionalism — sociological.)

6 It aids psychological adjustment of the individual by allowing him to project his hostility onto the ghosts, rather than turn it against himself and suffer acute anxiety. (Latent teleologic functionalism — psychobiological.)

7 It can be related to certain practices of infant and child care which produce great frustration in the child, whose consequent aggressions find institutional expression in this belief. (Latent genetic functionalism — ontogenetic.)

8 It is integrated with other kinds of institutionalized behaviour and attitude, such as sexual behaviour and attitudes. Since the malevolent

---

1 For a detailed analysis of the functions of this belief the reader is referred to Melford E. Spiro, 'Ghosts, Ifaluk and Teleological Functionalism.' *American Anthropologist*, 54:497-503, 1952, and 'Ghosts: An Anthropological Inquiry into Learning and Perception.' *Journal of Abnormal and Social Psychology*, 48:376-382, 1953.

ghosts attack primarily at night, and usually when an individual is alone, the Ifaluk rarely venture out at night, except for some religious ceremonial or public dance, but remain within the confines of their courtyard. Seemingly unrelated to this restriction on nocturnal mobility is the Ifaluk 'puritanical' attitude towards interaction — sexual or affectional — between adults of opposite sex. Husbands and wives, for example, sit apart in public; no embrace of any kind, even the holding of hands, is permitted lovers in public — indeed they never identify one another; love-making must take place in complete privacy, at the risk of suffering what, for the Ifaluk, is their greatest shame. The only privacy available for lovers is the 'bush', and it is in the bush, therefore, that lovers meet. But Ifaluk is a tiny atoll — a half a mile square. Should people normally take walks in the woods at night, or visit friends or relatives at night, lovers would have no privacy, and in the absence of privacy there can be no love-making. Hence we see how the belief in malevolent ghosts, nocturnal immobility, sexual attitudes, and sexual behaviour are integrated. (Latent configurational functionalism — social.)

We see, then, that this belief in malevolent ghosts can fall into nine of the twelve functionalist categories, so that a statement about the 'functionalism' of this — or any — belief remains almost meaningless, unless the exact usage of 'functionalism' is identified.

It should be understood, of course, that there is nothing in this typology which implies the necessity or universality of function. A functional analysis may discover non-functions or dysfunctions as readily as it discovers functions. A review of our categories reveals, however, that not all types of functional analysis will yield a functional-dysfunctional dichotomy. The teleologic category is most amenable to a dichotomous analysis, for here a functional institution is one which contributes to the welfare or survival of group or of individual; a dysfunctional institution, one which militates against the welfare or survival of the group and individual. On the other hand, for purposes of inter-, rather than intra-cultural analysis, it is possible to establish a functional-dysfunctional *continuum*. Since it is probably safe to say that all institutions have both functional and dysfunctional consequences, it would be possible to evaluate an economic or religious institution, for example, which is found in a number of cultures in terms of its relative position on a functional-dysfunctional continuum. This would make it possible to establish a quantitative scale for the measurement of teleologic function, and hence give us a basis for an objective comparative method.

'Configurational functionalism', on the other hand, always yields a functional-dysfunctional continuum, for here we are concerned with integration, and it is highly improbable that any culture is perfectly integrated or disintegrated. Thus both intra- and inter-cultural analysis could lead to generalizations about relative integration rather than absolute integration.

'Genetic functionalism', however, is not amenable at all to a functional-dysfunctional analysis. Here we are restricted to a functional-non-functional dichotomy, for our interest is in establishing a relationship between two institutions. If the relationship can be established, the institutions are 'functional' with respect to each other; if no relationship is established, the institutions are 'non-functional' with respect to each other. Thus, in an analysis of the Ifaluk belief in malevolent ghosts it was discovered that this belief has nine of the possible twelve functions of our typology, that it has three non-functions, and it has a number of dysfunctions.[1]

In summary, we see that the terms 'function' and 'functionalism' have been used in a number of quite different ways. All of them are useful, but difficulties can arise when the author does not state which use he is employing. An analysis of the various current usages of these terms, in theory and practice, reveals three bifurcated classes, which, in turn, can be broken down into manifest and latent functions; and these may be analyzed in terms of positive functions, non-functions, and dysfunctions.

Melford Spiro

---

1 The dysfunctions are summarized in Spiro, 1952, *op cit.*

A N

ACCOUNT

Of what happen'd in the

KINGDOM

O F

SWEDEN

In the Years 1669, and 1670 and upwards.

In Relation to ſome Perſons that were accuſed

For

Witches;

A N D

TRYED and EXECUTED

By the Kings Command.

Tranſlated out of High-Dutch into Engliſh,

By *Anthony Horneck* D. D.

Printed for *S. Lownds*, 1682.

A
RELATION
OF THE
Strange VVitchcraft
Difcovered in the
Village *Mobra* in *Swedeland,*

Taken out of the publick Regifter of the Lords Commiffioners appointed by his Majefty the King of Sweden *to examine the whole bufinefs, in the Years of our Lord 1669. and 1670.*

The News of this Witchcraft coming to the King's Ear, his Majesty was pleased to appoint Commissioners, some of the Clergy, and some of the Laity, to make a Journey to the Town aforesaid, and to examine the whole business; and accordingly the Examination was ordered to be on the 13th of August; and the Commissioners met on the 12th instant, in the said Village, at the Parson's House, to whom both the Minister and several people of fashion complained with tears in their Eyes, of the miserable condition they were in, and therefore begg'd of them to think of some way, whereby they might be delivered from that Calamity. They gave the Commissioners very strange Instances of the Devils Tyranny among them; how by the help of Witches, he had drawn some Hundreds of Children to him, and made them subject to his power; how he hath been seen to go in a visible shape through the Country, and appeared daily to the people; how he had wrought upon the poorer sort, by presenting them with Meat and Drink, and this way allured them to himself, with other circumstances to be mentioned hereafter. The Inhabitants of the Village added, with very great lamentations, that though their Children had told all, and themselves sought God very earnestly by

Prayer, yet they were carried away by him; and therefore begg'd of the Lords Commissioners to root out this hellish Crew, that they might regain their former rest and quietness; and the rather, because the Children which used to be carried away in the County or District of Elfdale, since some Witches had been burnt there, remained unmolested.

92 That day, *i.e.* the 13th of August, being the last Humiliation-day Instituted by Authority for removing of this Judgment, the Commissioners went to Church, where there appeared a considerable Assembly both of young and old: the Children could read most of them, and sing Psalms, and so could the Women, though not with any great zeal or fervor. There were preached two Sermons that day, in which the miserable case of those people, that suffered themselves to be deluded by the Devil, was laid open; and these Sermons were at last concluded with very fervent Prayer.

The Publick Worship being over, all the people of the Town were called together to the Parson's House, near Three thousand of them. Silence being Commanded, the King's Commission was read publickly in the hearing of them all, and they were charged under very great Penalties to conceal nothing of what they knew, and to say nothing but the truth; those especially, who were guilty, that the Children might be delivered from the Clutches of the Devil. They all promised obedience; the guilty feignedly, but the guiltless weeping and crying bitterly.

On the 14th of August the Commissioners met again, consulting how they might withstand this dangerous Flood; after long deliberation, an Order also coming from his Majesty, they did resolve to execute such, as the matter of fact could be proved upon; Examination being made, there were discovered no less than Three-score and ten in the Village aforesaid, Three and twenty of which freely confessing their Crimes, were condemned to dye; the rest, one pretending she was with Child, and the other denying and pleading not guilty, were sent to Fahluna, where most of them were afterwards Executed.

Fifteen Children which likewise confessed that they were engaged in this Witchery, died as the rest; Six and thirty of them between nine and sixteen years of age, who had been less guilty, were forced to run the Gantlet; Twenty more, who had no great inclination, yet had been seduced to those hellish Enterprizes, because they were very young, were Condemned to be lash'd with Rods upon their hands, for three Sundays together at the Church-door; and the aforesaid Six and thirty were also doom'd to be lash'd this way once a Week for a whole Year together. The number of the Seduced Children was about Three hundred.

On the twenty fifth of August, Execution was done upon the notoriously guilty, the day being bright and glorious, and the Sun shining, and some thousands of people being present at the Spectacle. The Order and Method observed in the Examination was thus:

First, The Commissioners and the Neighboring Justices went to Prayer; this done, the Witches, who had most of them Children with them, which they either had Seduced, or attempted to Seduce, from four years of age to sixteen, were set before them. Some of the Children complained lamentably of the misery and mischief they were forced sometime to suffer of the Witches.

The Children being asked whether they were sure, that they were at any time carried away by the Devil; they all declared they were, begging of the Commissioners that they might be freed from that intolerable Slavery.

Hereupon the Witches themselves were asked, whether the Confessions of these Children, were true, and admonished to confess the truth, that they might turn away from the Devil unto the living God. At first, most of them did very stifly, and without shedding the least Tear deny it, though much against their Will and Inclination.

After this, the Children were Examined, every one by themselves, to see whether their Confession did agree or no; and the Commissioners found that all of them, except some very little ones, who could not tell all the Circumstances, did punctually agree in the confession of Particulars.

In the mean while the Commissioners that were of the Clergy examined the Witches, but could not bring them to any Confession, all continuing steadfast in their denyals, till at last some of them burst out into Tears, and their Confession agreed with what the children had said. And these expressed their Abhorrency of the Fact, and begg'd pardon; adding, that the Devil, whom they call'd Loeyta, had stopt the Mouths of some of them, and stopt the Ears of others; and being now gone from them, they could no longer conceal it, for they now perceived his Treachery.

The Confession which the Witches made in Elfdale, to the Judges there, agreed with the Confession they made at Mohra: and the chief things they confessed consisted in these three Points.

1. Whither they used to go?

2. What kind of Place it was, they went to, called by them *Blockula,* where the Witches and the Devil used to meet.

3. What Evil or Mischief they had either done or designed there.

1. OF THEIR JOURNEY TO BLOCKULA. THE CONTENTS OF THEIR CONFESSION.

We of the Province of Elfdale, do confess that we used to go to a Gravel-pit which lay hard by a cross-way, and there we put on a Vest over our Heads, and then danced round, and after this ran to the Cross-way, and called the Devil thrice, first with a still Voice, the second time somewhat louder, and the third time very loud, with these Words, *Antecessour, come and carry us to* Blockula. Whereupon, immediately he used to appear, but in different Habits; but for the most part we saw him in a gray Coat, and red and blue Stockings: He had a red Beard, a high-crown'd Hat, with Linnen of divers Colours, wrapt about it, and long Garters upon his Stockings.

Then he asked us, if we would serve him with Soul and Body. If we were content to do so, he set us on a Beast which he had there ready, and carried us over Churches and high Walls; and after all we came to a green Meadow, where *Blockula* lies. We must procure some Scrapings of Altars, and Filings of Church-Clocks; and then he gives us a Horn with a Salve in it, wherewith we do anoint ourselves; and a Saddle, with a Hammer and a wooden Nail, thereby to fix the Saddle; whereupon we call upon the Devil and away we go.

Those that were of the Town of Mohra, made in a manner the same Declaration: Being asked whether they were sure of a real personal Transportation, and whether they were awake when it was done; they all answered in the Affirmative, and that the Devil sometimes laid something down in the Place that was very like them. But one of them confessed, that he did only take away her Strength, and her Body still lay upon the Ground; yet sometimes he took even her Body with him.

Being asked, how they could go with their Bodies through Chimneys and broken Panes of Glass, they said, that the Devil did first remove all that might hinder them in their flight, and so they had room enough to go.

Others were asked, how they were able to carry so many Children with them; and they answered, that when the Children were asleep they came into the Chamber, laid hold of the Children, which straightway did awake, and asked them whether they would go to a Feast with them? to which some answered Yes, others No; yet they were all forced to go. They only gave the Children a Shirt, a Coat, and a Doublet, which was either red or blue, and so they did set them upon a Beast of the Devil's providing, and then they rid away.

The Children confessed the same thing; and some added, that because they had very fine Cloaths put upon them, they were very willing to go.

Some of the Children concealed it from their Parents, but others discover'd it to them presently.

The Witches declared moreover, that till of late they never had the power to carry away Children, but only this Year and the last, and the Devil did at this time force them to it; that heretofore it was sufficient to carry but one of their Children, or a Stranger's Child with them, which yet happened seldom, but now he did plague them and whip them if they did not procure him Children, insomuch that they had no peace nor quiet for him; and whereas formerly one Journey a Week would serve turn, from their own Town to the place aforesaid, now they were forced to run to other Towns and Places for Children, and that they brought with them, some fifteen, some sixteen Children every night.

For their Journey, they said they made use of all sorts of Instruments, of Beasts, of Men, of Spits and Posts, according as they had opportunity: if they do ride upon Goats, and have many Children with them, that all may have Room, they stick a Spit into the back-side of the Goat, and then are anointed with the aforesaid Ointment. What the manner of their Journey is, God alone knows: Thus much was made out, That if the Children did at any time name the Names of those that had carried them away; they were again carried away by force either to *Blockula*, or to the Cross-ways, and there miserably beaten, insomuch that some of them died of it: and this some of the Witches confessed; and added, That now they were exceedingly troubled and tortured in their minds for it.

The Children thus used lookt mighty bleak, wan, and beaten. The marks of the Lashes, the Judges could not perceive in them, except in one Boy, who had some Wounds and Holes in his Back, that were given him with Thorns; but the Witches said, they would quickly vanish.

After this usage the Children are exceeding weak; and if any be carried over-night, they cannot recover themselves the next day; and they often fall into Fits, the coming of which they know by an extraordinary Paleness that seizes on the Children; and if a Fit comes upon them, they lean on their Mothers Arms, who sit up with them sometimes all night; and when they observe the Paleness coming, shake the Children, but to no purpose.

They observe further, that their Childrens Breasts grow cold at such times; and they take sometimes a burning Candle and stick it in their hair, which yet is not burnt by it. They swoun upon this Paleness, which Swoun lasteth sometimes half an hour, sometimes an hour, sometimes two hours, and when the Children come to themselves again, they mourn and lament, and groan most miserably, and beg exceedingly to be eased: This two old Men declared upon Oath before the Judges, and called all the Inhabitants of the Town to witness, as Persons that had most of them experience of this strange Symptome of their Children.

A little Girl of Elfdale confessed, That naming the name of JESUS as she was carried away, she fell suddenly upon the Ground, and got a great hole in her Side, which the Devil presently healed up again, and away he carried her; and to this day the Girl confessed, she had exceeding great pain in her Side.

Another Boy confessed too, That one day he was carried away by his Mistress, and to perform the Journey, he took his own Fathers Horse out of the Meadow where it was, and upon his return, she let the Horse go in her own ground.

The next Morning the Boys Father sought for his Horse, and not finding it, gave it over for lost; but the Boy told him the whole story, and so his Father fetcht the Horse back again; and this one of the Witches confessed.

2. OF THE PLACE WHERE THEY USED TO ASSEMBLE, CALLED BLOCKULA, AND WHAT THEY DID THERE.

They unanimously confessed, that *Blockula* is situated in a delicate large Meadow, whereof you can see no end. The place or House they met at, had before it a Gate painted with divers Colours; through this Gate they went into a little Meadow distinct from the other, where the Beasts went, that they used to ride on: But the Men whom they made use of in their Journey, stood in the House by the Gate in a slumbering posture, sleeping against the Wall.

In a huge large Room of this House, they said, there stood a very long Table, at which the Witches did sit down; And that hard by this Room was another Chamber, where there were very lovely and delicate Beds.

The first thing they said, they must do at *Blockula*, was, That they must deny all, and devote themselves Body and Soul to the Devil, and promise to serve him faithfully, and confirm all this with an Oath. Hereupon they cut their Fingers, and with their Bloud writ their Name in his Book. They added, that he caused them to be Baptized too by such Priests as he had there, and made them confirm their Baptism with dreadful Oaths and Imprecations.

Hereupon the Devil gave them a Purse, wherein there were filings of Clocks with a Stone tied to it, which they threw into the Water, and then were forced to speak these words; *As these filings of the Clock do never return to the Clock from which they are taken, so may my Soul never return to Heaven.* To which they add Blasphemy and other Oaths and Curses.

The mark of their cut Fingers is not found in all of them: But a girl who had been slashed over her Finger, declared, that because she would not stretch out her Finger, the Devil in anger had so cruelly wounded it.

After this they sate down to Table; and those that the Devil esteemed most, were placed nearest to him; but the Children must stand at the door, where he himself gives them Meat and Drink.

The Diet they did use to have there, was, they said, Broth with Colworts and Bacon in it, Oatmeal, Bread spread with Butter, Milk, and Cheese. And they added, that sometimes it tasted very well, and sometimes very ill. After Meals they went to Dancing, and in the mean while Swore and Cursed most dreadfully, and afterward went to fighting one with another.

Those of Elfdale confessed, That the Devil used to play upon an Harp before them, and afterwards to go with them that he liked best, into a Chamber, where he committed venerous Acts with them; and this indeed all confessed, That he had carnal knowledge of them, and that the Devil had Sons and Daughters by them, which he did Marry together, and they did couple, and brought forth Toads and Serpents.

One day the Devil seemed to be dead, whereupon there were great lamentations at *Blockula;* but he soon awaked again. If he hath a mind to be merry with them, he lets them all ride upon Spits before him; takes afterwards the Spits and beats them black and blue, and then laughs at them. And he bids them believe, that the day of Judgment will come speedily, and therefore sets them to work to build a great House of Stone, promising, that in that House he will preserve them from God's Fury, and cause them to enjoy the greatest Delights and Pleasures: but while they work exceedingly hard at it, there falls a great part of the Wall down again, whereby some of the Witches are commonly hurt which makes him laugh, but presently he cures them again.

They said, they had seen sometimes a very great Devil like a Dragon, with Fire round about him, and bound with an Iron Chain; and the Devil, that converses with them tells them, that if they confess any thing, he will let that great Devil loose upon them, whereby all Sweedland shall come into great danger.

They added, That the Devil had a Church there, such another as in the Town of Mohra. When the Commissioners were coming he told the

Witches, they should not fear them; for he would certainly kill them all. And they confessed, that some of them had attempted to murder the Commissioners, but had not been able to effect it.

Some of the Children talked much of a white Angel, which used to forbid them what the Devil had bid them do, and told them that those doings would not last long: what had been done was permitted because of the Wickedness of the People, and the carrying away of the Children should be made manifest. And they added, that this white Angel would place Himself sometimes at the Door betwixt the Witches and the Children; and when they came to *Blockula*, he pulled the Children back, but the Witches they went in.

3. OF THE MISCHIEF OR EVIL WHICH THE WITCHES PROMISED TO DO TO MEN AND BEASTS.

They confessed, that they were to promise the Devil, that they would do all that's Ill; and that the Devil taught them to Milk, which was in this wise: They used to stick a Knife in the Wall, and hang a kind of Label on it, which they drew and stroaked; and as long as this lasted, the Persons that they had power over were miserably plagued, and the Beasts were milked that way, till sometimes they died of it.

A Woman confessed, that the Devil gave her a wooden Knife, wherewith, going into Houses, she had power to kill any thing, she touched with it; yet there were few, that would confess, that they had hurt any Man or Woman.

Being asked whether they had murthered any Children, they confessed, that they had indeed tormented many, but did not know, whether any of them died of those Plagues. And added, That the Devil had shewed them several Places, where he had power to do Mischief.

The Minister of Elfdale, declared, That one Night these Witches, were to his thinking, upon the crown of his Head, and that from thence he had had a long continued Pain of the Head.

One of the Witches confessed too, that the Devil had sent her to torment that Minister: and that she was ordered to use a Nail and strike it into his Head, but it would not enter very deep; and thence came that Headache.

The aforesaid Minister said also, That one Night he felt a Pain, as if he were torn with an Instrument, that they cleanse Flax with, or a Flax-comb; and when he waked, he heard somebody scratching and scraping, at the Window, but could see no-body. And one of the Witches confessed, that she was the Person that did it, being sent by the Devil.

The Minister of Mohra declared also, that one Night one of these Witches came into his House, and did so violently take him by the Throat, that he thought, he should have been choaked; and waking, he saw the Person that did it, but could not know her; and that for some Weeks he was not able to speak, or perform Divine Service.

An old Woman of Elfdale confessed, that the Devil had holpen her to make a Nail, which she struck into a Boy's knee, of which Stroke the Boy remained lame a long time. And she added, that before she burnt, or was executed by the hand of Justice, the Boy would recover.

They confessed also, that the Devil gives them a Beast about the bigness and shape of a young Cat, which they call a *Carrier*; and that he gives them a Bird too as big as a Raven, but white. And these two Creatures they can send any where; and where-ever they come, they take away all sorts of Victuals they can get, Butter, Cheese, Milk, Bacon, and all sorts of Seeds whatever they find, and carry it to the Witch. What the Bird brings they may keep for themselves; but what the Carrier brings, they must reserve for the Devil, and that's brought to *Blockula*, where he doth give them of it so much as he thinks fit.

They added likewise, that these Carriers fill themselves so full sometimes, that they are forced to spue by the way, which spueing is found in several Gardens where Colworts grow, and not far from the Houses of those Witches. It is of a yellow colour like Gold, and is called *Butter of Witches.*

The Lords Commissioners were indeed very earnest, and took great Pains to perswade them to shew some of their Tricks, but to no purpose; for they did all unanimously confess, that since they had confessed all, they found that all their Witchcraft was gone, and that the Devil at this time appeared to them very terrible, with Claws on his Hands and Feet, and with Horns on his Head, and a long Tail behind, and shewed to them a Pit burning, with a Hand put out; but the Devil did thrust the Person down again with an Iron-fork; and suggested to the Witches, that if they continued in their Confession, he would deal with them in the same manner.

The abovesaid Relation is taken out of the Publick Register, where all this is related with more Circumstances. And at this time through all the Countrey there are Prayers weekly in all Churches, to the end that Almighty God would pull down the Devil's Power, and deliver those poor Creatures, which have hitherto groaned under it.

FREUD AND THE HUCKSTERS

Seduced by the advertising industry, an increasing number of social scientists are turning into super-hucksters. Today any number of psychologists and sociologists will gladly undertake to probe the mass mind to discover, for instance, how non-drinkers can be persuaded to drink and drinkers to drink more. They only want a fat check — which they get.

To understand this strange marriage between salesmanship and the social sciences, one must view it against the background of our merchandising system. Advertising's single function is to sell the goods produced by industry. A successful advertising agency must therefore conduct extensive market research. In agencies of any size a special department collects all kinds of data on the markets open to clients' products and on consumers' reactions to both products and advertising.

In this task it uses the work done by the pollsters. Roper, Gallup, Crossley, and the others do not depend for their livelihood, as some may think, on political forecasting but on market surveys done for business. In fact, the whole range of statistical research and opinion sampling got its first impetus from business concerns which felt the need of reliable data on markets and consumer attitudes.

Sociology and psychology have recently come in for increased attention on the theory that if an advertising man can gain a better understanding of human behaviour, he will be able to turn out copy with more 'sell' appeal. Of course advertising has always used this approach in a haphazard, intuitive manner. Deodorants, soaps, and toothpastes have been sold through an appeal to such human emotions as love, fear, ambition, and the desire to be popular. Commercial use of facts discovered by the social sciences has long been advocated by certain psychologists, notably Ernest Dichter and the late Henry C. Link; as far back as 1919 Link was acting as psychological consultant to the United States Rubber Company. A number of advertising agencies have quietly but consciously employed these techniques for more than a decade.

Today the application of the social sciences to advertising has become a veritable fad. McCann-Erickson, one of the five top agencies in the United States, has its own psychological-research staff. Weiss and Geller, a large Chicago agency, holds regular staff conferences with prominent social scientists; Edward Weiss, president of the agency, believes the social sciences will 'revolutionize' advertising. The lead article in the fall *Journal of Marketing* described the various schools of psychology and made suggestions about how their concepts could be used in marketing. The Chicago *Tribune's* Distribution and Advertising Forum in 1952 took as one of its three basic topics the role that the social sciences can play in advertising and selling. At the annual convention of the American Marketing Association held in Chicago at the end of December, the social sciences stole the show, getting front-page play in the *Wall Street Journal* and *Advertising Age*.

How, specifically, are the techniques of the social sciences being utilized in advertising? A brief account of a few typical advertising campaigns will make the procedure fairly clear.

WHY DO PEOPLE CHEW GUM?

The Wrigley Gum Company wanted to know, and Weiss and Geller undertook to find the answer. A study made at the Institute of Psychoanalysis in Chicago produced three reasons – for oral comfort, for release of tension, to express symbolic hostility or aggression. The advertising agency next made a comprehensive sociological survey of a coal-mining area in eastern Pennsylvania, where gum sales were well below the national level. It discovered that the area had a relatively high rate of illiteracy, a large foreign-born population, and a low standard of living.

Putting the results of the two studies together, Weiss and Geller laid out a campaign for this particular region. The theme was frustration and the relief obtained by chewing gum. The idea was presented on a series of comic-strip ads. The first showed a child unable to do a simple, everyday task and overcoming his difficulty after an adult gave him a stick of gum. A second showed adults conquering frustration in the same way. The strips used a minimum of words so as to avoid the impression of insincerity and reach a not too literate public. During the year that the campaign ran, Wrigley reported that the sales in the test area increased at a much higher rate than in the rest of the country. As a result the campaign was expanded to fourteen other markets.

WHY DO PEOPLE DRINK?

McCann-Erickson explored this question by interviewing people while they were drinking. The results seemed to divide drinkers into two main groups—those who drink as a means of retreat, and those who drink for the effect. The agency felt it could not project the first group in an ad in terms of a social situation. Its analysis of the second group revealed that the heavy drinkers drink either because it makes them feel better, helps them overcome their shyness, and so on or because they 'become able to think independently and to use their creative ability'. Another finding was that drinkers tend to associate the taste of liquor with the effect produced.

Since previous market research had showed that heavy drinkers consume 80 per cent of the hard liquor sold, McCann-Erickson decided that effective liquor advertising should 'feature a taste promise which had an effect connotation' and 'the types of drinks popular among heavy drinkers'. Two McCann-Erickson clients who might be interested in this study are Melrose Distillers and Schenley Distillers.

WHY DO PEOPLE SMOKE?

This question was investigated by Social Research, Inc., which discovered the following reasons: cigarettes relieve tension, express sociability, aid poise, help anticipate stress, give sensory pleasure, are proof of daring, are signs of sophistication, help discharge energy, and signify conformity.

Advertising is important, Social Research stressed, because it popularizes a brand and smokers want to think their brand is popular. Advertising thus helps to make smoking 'respectable'. But the problem of all cigarette advertising, Social Research told the manufacturers, is how to combine a pleasure promise with reassurances that the tobacco will not hurt you. The solution advanced by Social Research was the generalization: 'Cigarette advertising calls for creativity, for new departures, for an invitation to smoke that is not just a variation of assertions that "you like it" or "it won't hurt you".'

Other special psychological tests being used today in marketing have to do with 'thematic apperception', word association, Rorschach ink blots, and Rosenzweig picture frustration. One company, the Ad Detector Research Corporation of Chicago, even uses the galvanometer, or lie detector. Consumers are strapped to the machine, ads are flashed before their eyes, and as they comment, their reactions are recorded. The Chicago *Tribune* has made this copy-testing service available to its advertisers at a cost of $75 per ad.

A number of concerns have profited greatly from this tendency to base advertising on sociological and psychological studies. The Psychological Corporation, founded thirty years ago in New York, lost money for some time, but with advertisers' acceptance of psychological research, its income rose from $250,000 in 1939 to $1,500,000 in 1951. Today more than half of its earnings comes from business and industry. The head of the Institute for Research in Mass Motivations, Dr. Ernest Dichter, a Vienna-born psychologist, began by helping the Chrysler Corporation to sell Plymouths through a socio-psychological advertising approach in 1937. Since then, he has, in his own words, 'conducted research and completed more than 300 surveys in almost every field of selling and for almost every type of product'.

It should be pointed out here that the social scientists engaged in market research are not of the pseudo variety. Many are ranking authorities in their fields. For example, among the present directors of Psychological Corporation are Robert Thorndike, professor of education at Columbia University; Robert S. Woodworth, professor emeritus of psychology at Columbia; Donald G. Marquis, chairman of the Department of Psychology at the University of Michigan; and Walter R. Miles, professor of psychology at Yale. The executive director of Social Research, Inc., in Chicago is Burleigh Gardner, a former University of Chicago professor and co-author of *Deep South*. Dr. Gardner as teacher and scholar contributed greatly to our understanding of class differences in American culture. Recently he addressed the American Marketing Association on the topic, 'Putting Stereotypes and Prejudices to Work in Your Advertising Strategy'. Drawing on his knowledge of American society he warned advertisers that the right stereotype must be used for each economic and social group: in ads intended for *Ebony* a Negro model must be used; an ad designed for the *New Yorker* will not have the maximum impact on readers of *True Detective*.

The role played by social science in advertising raises the issue of the social scientist's place in society. Often, pleading 'objectivity', he chooses to remain aloof from the social struggle. But his work shows that he stands for social and economic reform. His studies have inevitably led him to take the position, at least on the abstract level, that the structure of society, not human nature, is responsible for such ills as poverty and discrimination. It is ironic, then, to find sociologists and psychologists – most of whom know the score on social and economic inequalities – offering their services for projects whose aim is to increase sales through the manipulation of legitimate consumer desires. If the social scientist becomes the hireling of advertising and business, how can he study objectively their social implications?

Social scientists in the past have paid attention to the irrational patterns of human behaviour because they wish to locate their social origins and thus be able to suggest changes that would result in more rational conduct. They now study irrationality – and other aspects of human behaviour – to gather data that may be used by salesmen to manipulate consumers. No one, except perhaps Mr. Wrigley, can believe that chewing gum will relieve the basic frustrations of Pennsylvania coal miners.

The entrance of bona fide social scientists into the field of marketing is all the more shocking in view of the known damaging effects on personality of advertising which stimulates desires but offers no real means of satisfying them. The late Karen Horney, in *The Neurotic Personality of Our Time*, referred to this danger:

> For economic reasons needs are constantly being stimulated in our culture by such means as advertisements, 'conspicuous consumption', the ideal of 'keeping up with the Joneses'. For the great majority, however, the actual fulfilment of these needs is closely restricted. The psychic consequence for the individual is a constant discrepancy between his desires and their fulfilment.

The sales executive, however, looks upon the public – his market – as an uninformed mass of people in whom certain desires must be aroused to get them to part with their money. The assumption of the business man is almost always that the public has the necessary purchasing power but for some ridiculous reason – such as insecurity – does not want to use it.

There is already evidence that the qualitative researchers plan to extend their operations beyond selling to the manipulation of public opinion on political questions. In 1951 the Psychological Corporation tested the effectiveness of a comic book 'designed for the economic education of industrial workers'. Entitled *How Stalin Hopes We Will Destroy America*, the book was distributed to a group of factory workers, and 'its impact was tested in terms of ideas left with readers and attitudes affected'. The results indicated, the research concern reported, that 'the booklet had an educational effect'. It was therefore sponsored by an industrial client, who has distributed 800,000 copies to date. Ernest Dichter, in a series of talks he gave before the 1952 Presidential election, predicted that the campaign issues — Korea, inflation, corruption — would have little to do with the outcome. The decisive factor, according to Dichter, would be the emotional appeal exercised by the candidates. After the election Burleigh Gardner said in a letter to *Tide*, a news weekly for the advertising industry:

I do think it is time to apply fresh techniques to the problem of political predictions. We believe that the strong Eisenhower majority could have been predicted using projection techniques. You could probably predict from the underlying emotional tone rather than from conscious beliefs.

Dichter's and Gardner's statements come under the heading of sales promotion. For the two men are in a competitive business. They must vie with the Gallups and Ropers to get orders from business, and they want to be in the first row when political groups decide to approach the problem of voter manipulation in the same 'scientific' manner in which business now approaches selling problems. It would be a mistake to assume that the sociologists and psychologists who are helping to sell soaps and cigarettes are above this kind of opinion molding.

Ralph Goodman

NOT FOR CHILDREN

The American generation born since 1930 cannot read. It has not learned, it will not learn, and it does not need to. Reading ability just sufficient to spell out the advertisements is all that is demanded in our culture. With only token recourse to the printed word, for more than a decade the radio, the talking movie, the picture-magazine and comic-book have served all the cultural and recreational needs of the generation of adults now upon us. For them, the printed word is on its way out.

Increasingly, in the last century, sadism has been supplied to the American public in massive doses in all its popular arts until, now, one out of every three trees cut down in Canada for paper-pulp has murder printed on it when the presses roll. The frustrations – sexual and economic – that this printed violence has been siphoning off, will obviously not disappear along with the ability to read. And so, new aural and visual media have been prepared, primed to replace the murder-mystery and 'action' pulp now turning dim before the eyes of a growing nation of illiterates. Whole industries have sprung up based ultimately on the exchanging of printed death for pictorial. The murder movie, the radio horror show, the bloody sports that have put television over, the disaster headlines of the daily tabloids and the photographic agonies of the weekly, *Life* [sic] and its various imitators, all are chomping at the bit—ready, willing, and anxious to purvey 'cathartic' violence to trapped millions. The kiddies' korner in this new national welter of blood is the comic-book. The hood, the disguise, the Ku Klux promise of immunity: 'entertainment'.

The aggressive content of comic-books is so conspicuous that most observers fail to notice that this aggression is rigidly channelized, that the willingness of any reader to accept a fantasy escape from his frustrations presupposes a willingness to achieve something less than total and actual escape. Like all other forms of dreaming, literature operates under censorship. And this censorship — in both its legal and internalized expression — does not allow any direct, total attack on the frustration that elicits the dream. It offers a choice. Either the attack must restrict itself to something less than an attack, to partial and symbolic aggressions, or its object must appear in disguise.

In practice this adds up to a choice between fantasy attacks on real frustrations, and real attacks on fantasy frustrations. This is also the difference between comic-strips and comic-books: not to be confused. The strips published in newspapers are for adults, and concentrate on real enemies — husbands, wives, bosses, policemen, and civilized pressures in general. With equal realism, they restrict this attack to mere permissible comedy — to pranks, jeers, and naughtiness: token resistance.

The comic-*books* are for children, and their content is totally that of dreams. They concentrate on impossibly real aggressions — impossible under civilized restraints — with fists, guns, torture, whips, and blood. Meanwhile, the dream-censorship respectabilizes this attack by directing it against some scapegoat criminal or wild animal, or even against some natural law like gravity, rather than against the parents and teachers who are the real sources of the child's frustration and therefore the real objects of his aggression.

Children are not allowed to fantasy themselves as actually revolting against authority — as actually killing their fathers — nor a wife as actually killing her husband. A literature frankly offering images for such fantasies would be outlawed overnight. But, in the identifications available in comic-strips — in the character of the Katzenjammer Kids, in the kewpie-doll character of Blondie—both father and husband can be thoroughly beaten up, harassed, humiliated, and degraded daily. Lulled by these halfway aggressions — that is to say, halfway to murder — the censorship demands only that in the final sequence Hans & Fritz must submit to flagellation for their 'naughtiness', Blondie to the inferior position of being, after all, merely a wife. In other words, the *status quo* must be restored in some perfunctory genuflection as the reader leaves. This is the contract under which direct-attack fantasy is allowed: the attack must be incomplete; even so, being against authority, it must be punished; and, in the last analysis, it must change nothing.

Obviously this is unsatisfactory. Adults, habituated to compromise, can make their peace with it, but for children it is apparently intolerable. Not only the degree of allowed violence is much too low, but the final punishment reinstates, as it is meant to reinstate, precisely the situation the child is trying to escape from. Children's literature, therefore — the really popular children's literature: Grimm's *Fairy Tales,* the expurgated *Arabian Nights,* Foxe's *Book of Martyrs,* and now the comic-book — traditionally takes the other alternative, disguising the hated parent and feared authority (necessarily sacrosanct) as a witch, an ogre, a pirate, Red Indian, clay duck, criminal, martyr, spy, saboteur, 'mad' scientist, or other human sacrifice condemned to die by definition; and in this way becomes free to enact upon him — or her — a really satisfactory degree of violence. At the same unconscious level that the reader identifies himself with the heroic avenger, he may also identify whoever has been frustrating him with the corpse.

Violence displaced in this way from its intended object invariably appears in larger and larger doses, more and more often repeated. Little trapped people, who have no other medicine but the wrong one, can be expected to take more and more of it, to still the growing realization that they will never be cured that way. At this point, what was intended as social antisepsis becomes pathology. Not knowing, or not being able to admit that they are fobbed off with scapegoats, children are nevertheless aware that their transvalued violence does not satisfy them. They keep asking for more. Increase the dose! Twenty years ago, in 1933, there was not one comic-book openly published in the United States. In 1948, at a conservative estimate, there were five hundred million yearly: three hundred titles or more, each with an average monthly printing of two hundred thousand copies. From zero to half a billion, in fifteen years — the greatest, fastest literary success the world has ever seen.

The history of the comic-book has not yet been traced. Its descent can be roughly seen in the bison-drawings of the cave-dwellers, the hieroglyphic writings of Egypt (in which the *cartouche,* or conversation-balloon, first appears), the architectural friezes of Babylonia, Central America and Indonesia, the ceramic decorations of Greece, the silver-chasing of Roman arms and armour, the wall *graffiti* of Pompeii (and compare our own), the hunting tapestries of the Middle Ages, the playing-cards, fortune-telling Tarot and pious block-books of the Renaissance, the woodcut Dances of Death of 15th century France, the horizontal scrolls (*maki-*

mono) and picture-books of Japan, the crowded canvases of the Flemish peasant painters Breughel, Brouwer, and Bosch.

The modern comic-book had been achieved in Hogarth's *Harlot's Progress* (1732), in Rodolphe Topffer's *Histories* – pirated in the 1840's as the first American comic-books (*American Notes & Queries*, 1946, vol. 5: page 149) – and, in full colour and all, in *The Fools Paradise* published by Hotten in London about 1873; but only the strips flourished until the 1930's. There, in the private lynchings of detective 'Dick Tracy' and 'Secret Agent X-9' (by way of Edgar Allan Poe), the interplanetary paranoia of 'Buck Rogers' and 'Flash Gordon' (H. G. Wells' *War of the Worlds*, 1898) and the loincloth cavortings of 'Jungle Jim' (Edgar Rice Burroughs' *Tarzan*, 1914), a formula was evolved that restored the comics to children at least on Sundays – the daily strips having been abandoned by them to adults a decade before, as too unbearably tame.

Im tiefsten Depressionzeit, with money-anxieties and the fear of war hanging over the American mind, it was not difficult to peddle a cult of death, with the reader finding identification naturally in the topmost killer. Murder-mysteries boomed. Cowboy pulps blossomed, in both their western and interplanetary avatars. And for children, the Mars and crime and jungle strips showed that it was possible to go beyond Mr. Hearst's Katzenjammer Kids and their pea-shooter (plagiarized to order from Wilhelm Busch's 'Max und Moritz', half a century before), and really handle guns and blood.

By 1936, before anyone had even heard of the comic-books then preparing, a sociologist could find the Sunday strips 'catering to neurosis', offering 'escape to a morbid imagery and brutal sadism',[1] while from the Catholic University in Washington came this résumé of the contents of, mind you, strips:

> Sadism, cannibalism, bestiality. Crude eroticism. Torturing, killing, kidnapping . . . Monsters, madmen, creatures half-brute, half-human. Raw melodrama; tales of crime and criminals . . . pirate stories . . . emphasis upon cruelty, human torture, horrible forms of death, human sacrifice . . . repetition in word and picture of . . . bestial and degenerate scenes. . . .[2]

with a few bitter animadversions on the spectacle of the Supreme Court of the United States sitting gravely upon the 'momentous issue, who would purvey these scenes to the people of the District of Columbia', in bland disregard of the principle that contestants must come into court with clean hands, that there can be no equity in a *prima facie* immoral act.

Then came the comic-books, the secret of their unprecedented success – if anything can be called a secret that appears in sixty million copies

1 Aaron Berkman, in *American Spectator*, 4:53, 1936.
2 John K. Ryan, in *Forum*, 95:301-304, 1936.

monthly — being, of course, their violence. All comic-books without exception are principally, if not wholly, devoted to violence. And just as the murder-stories for the use of frustrated adults are politely euphemised as 'mysteries', just so the yearly half-billion violence-leaflets for children are camouflaged as 'funnies', as 'comics', as 'jokes', though there is never anything comical in them.

110 Garishly presented in clashing colours, and cheaply printed in forty-eight pages of paper-bound pulp with even more garish covers, what recourse there is in comic-books to the printed word is, totally, language violence: full capitals throughout, bold-face accents liberally besprinkled, and exclamation points galore; with illiterate little cartouches, where no conversation is thought necessary, saying *Pow, Zow,* and *Whammo!* to indicate the administration of violence, while the victims respond with *Awrrk, Aagh, Aiee, Ooof,* and *Uggh.*

The price being only ten cents apiece, and the distribution national, every American child can and does read from ten to a dozen of these pamphlets monthly, an unknown number of times, and then trades them off for others. If there is only one violent picture per page — and there are usually more — this represents a minimum supply, to every child old enough to look at pictures, of three hundred scenes of beating, shooting, strangling, torture, and blood per month, or ten a day if he reads each comic-book only once. The fortification of this visual violence with precisely similar aural violence over the radio daily, and both together in the movies on Saturday, must also be counted in.

With rare exceptions, every child in America who was six years old in 1938 had, by 1948, absorbed an absolute minimum of eighteen thousand pictorial beatings, shootings, stranglings, blood-puddles, and torturings-to-death, from comic (ha-ha) books alone, identifying himself — unless he is a complete masochist — with the heroic beater, shooter, strangler, blood-letter, and-or torturer in every case. With repetition like that, you can teach a child anything: that black is white, to stand on his head, eat hair — anything. At the moment it is being used to teach him — and in no quiet professorial tone, but rather in flaming colour and superheated dialogue — that violence is heroic, and murder a red-hot thriller.

The effect, if not the intention, has been to raise up an entire generation of adolescents — twenty million of them — who have felt, thousands upon thousands of times, all the sensations and emotions of committing murder, except pulling the trigger. And toy guns and fireworks, advertised in the back pages of the comics — cap-shooters, b-b rifles (with manufacturer's enscrolled Bill of Rights), paralysis pistols, crank'em-up tommyguns, six-inch cannon-crackers, and ray-gats emitting a spark a foot and a half long — have supplied that. The Universal Military Training of the mind.

The theory on which we supply corpses to children, as playthings, is not a secret. If it is generally cloaked in the Aristotelian fustian of 'tragic catharsis', and seldom put into plain words, it is because it does not make good listening. It is this: We train children as we train other animals, by breaking their spirit. We fit them, not for the life they are prepared for as they emerge from the womb – and no one has ever bothered to find out what that natural human life is – but rather for a very different civilized life, forced upon them ready-made by adults. The child's natural character – again, whatever it may be – must be distorted to fit civilization, just as his feet must be distorted to fit shoes. This is called education, and naturally the child resists it. But by feeding him blood he can be drugged into acquiescence while we break his spirit, distort his bones and his character, and, in a word, civilize him. Fantasy violence will paralyse his resistance, divert his aggression to unreal enemies and frustrations, and in this way prevent him from rebelling against parents and teachers busy abnormalizing him. When he grows up, the human sacrifices will be continued in all the popular arts with paid or accidental victims – as in prize-fights and headlines – and this will siphon off his resistance against society, and prevent revolution. At any rate, that is the theory. And if we accept the premise that the civilized life is better than the natural and worth distorting children to fit, there is no arguing with the methods that do the job. The method being blood, feed children blood.

Baldly stated – and I hope it is bald enough – that is the standard psychiatric justification for comic-books. Now let's examine it. Accept, for the moment, the premise that though we have more jails than we have high-schools, more insane-asylums than colleges, by some criterion our society can be called successful and ought to be kept going. But does the let-'em-eat-blood theory really work? Historically it has always failed. The gladiatorial arena did not save Rome. Instead, the breadmasters and slaves saw played before their eyes their own coming dissolution. The surfeit of death in the blood-drama of Marlowe and Shakespeare and Kyd did not avert the English Revolution. The Black Hundreds' butchering of Jews did not avert the Russian. The incinerating of six million more Jews in Germany did not preserve the Nazi régime. To the contrary, where institutionalized violence appears in history, it is as the last resort of bankrupt civilizations, sick and reeling unto death.

The admission, so cheerfully made, that children *need* these aggressive outlets in fantasy against their parents, teachers, policemen, and total social environment is an admission that this social environment does not have a place for the child. The necessity for the same outlet by adults then means that the social environment has no place in it for adults. For whom has the social environment a place?

G. Legman

CULTURE WITHOUT LITERACY

The ordinary desire of everybody to have everybody else think alike with himself has some explosive implications today. The perfection of the *means* of communication has given this average power-complex of the human being an enormous extension of expression.

The telephone, the teleprinter and the wireless made it possible for orders from the highest levels to be given direct to the lowest levels, where, on account of the absolute authority behind them, they were carried out uncritically; or brought it about that numerous offices and command çentres were directly connected with the supreme leadership from which they received their sinister orders without any intermediary; or resulted in a widespread surveillance of the citizen, or in a high degree of secrecy surrounding criminal happenings. To the outside observer this governmental apparatus may have resembled the apparently chaotic confusion of lines at a telephone exchange, but like the latter it could be controlled and operated from one central source. Former dictatorships needed collaborators of high quality even in the lower levels of leadership, men who could think and act independently. In the era of modern technique an authoritarian system can do without this. The means of communication alone permit it to mechanize the work of subordinate leadership. As a consequence a new type develops: the uncritical recipient of orders.[1]

Perfection of the *means* of communication has meant instantaneity. Such an instantaneous network of communication is the body-mind unity of each of us. When a city or a society achieves a diversity and equilibrium of awareness analogous to the body-mind network, it has what we tend to regard as a high culture.

But the instantaneity of communication makes free speech and thought difficult if not impossible and for many reasons. Radio extends the range of the casual speaking voice, but it forbids that many should speak. And when what is said has such range of control it is forbidden to speak any but the most acceptable words and notions. Power and control are in all cases paid for by loss of freedom and flexibility.

Today the entire globe has a unity in point of mutual inter-awareness which exceeds in rapidity the former flow of information in a small city – say Elizabethan London with its eighty or ninety thousand inhabitants. What happens to existing societies when they are brought into such intimate contact by press, picture stories, news-reels and jet propulsion? What happens when the neolithic Eskimo is compelled to share the time and space arrangements of technological man? What happens in our minds as we become familiar with the diversity of human cultures which have come into existence under innumerable circumstances, historical and geographical? Is not what happens comparable to that social revolution which we call the American melting-pot?

When the telegraph made possible a daily cross-section of the globe transferred to the page of newsprint, we already had our mental melting-pot for cosmic man – the world citizen. The mere format of the page of newsprint was more revolutionary in its intellectual and emotional consequences than anything that could be *said* about any part of the globe.

When we juxtapose news items from Tokio, London, New York, Chile, Africa and New Zealand we are not just manipulating space. The events so brought together belong to cultures widely separated in time. The modern world abridges all historical times as readily as it reduces space. Every*where* and every *age* have become *here* and *now*. History has been abolished by our new media. If prehistoric man is simply preliterate man living in a timeless world of seasonal recurrence, may not posthistoric man find himself in a similar situation? May not the upshot of our technology be the awakening from the historically conditioned nightmare of the past

[1] Albert Speer, German Armament Minister in 1942, in a speech at the Nuremburg trials, quoted in Hjalmar Schacht, *Account Settled*, London, 1949, p. 240.

into a timeless present? Historic man may turn out to have been literate man. An episode.

Robert Redfield in his recent book *The Primitive World and Its Transformations* points to the timeless character of preliterate societies where exclusively oral communication ensures intimacy, homogeneity and fixity of social experience. It is the advent of writing that sets in motion the urban revolution. Writing breaks up the fixity and homogeneity of preliterate societies. Writing creates that inner dialogue or dialectic, that psychic withdrawal which makes possible the reflexive analysis of thought via the stasis of the audible made spatial. Writing is the translation of the audible into the spatial as reading is the reverse of this reciprocal process. And the complex shuttling of eye, ear and speech factors once engaged in this ballet necessarily reshape the entire communal life, both inner and outer, creating not only the 'stream of consciousness' rediscovered by contemporary art, but ensuring multiple impediments to the activities of perception and recall.

So far as writing is the spatializing and arrest of oral speech, however, it implies that further command of space made possible by the written message and its attendant road system. With writing, therefore, comes logical analysis and specialism, but also militarism and bureaucracy. And with writing comes the break in that direct, intuitive relationship between men and their surroundings which modern art has begun to uncover.

'Compared with the evidence afforded by living tradition,' says Sir James Frazer, 'the testimony of ancient books on the subject of the early religion is worth very little. For literature accelerates the advance of thought at a rate which leaves the slow progress of opinion by word of mouth at an immeasurable distance behind. Two or three generations of literature may do more to change thought than two or three thousand years of traditional life.'[1] But literature, as we know today, is a relatively conservative time-binding medium compared with press, radio and movie. So the thought is now beginning to occur: How many thousands of years of change can we afford every ten years? May not a spot of culture-lag here and there in the great time-flux prove to be a kind of social and psychological oasis?

Involved with the loss of memory and the psychic withdrawal of alphabetic cultures, there is a decline of sensuous perception and adequacy of social responsiveness. The preternatural sensuous faculties of Sherlock Holmes or the modern sleuth are simply those of preliterate man who can retain the details of a hundred-mile trail as easily as a movie camera can

---

[1] J. Frazer, *Man, God and Immortality*, 1927, p. 318.

record it. Today our detailed knowledge of societies existing within the oral tradition enables us to estimate accurately the advantages and disadvantages of writing. Without writing there is little control of space, but perfect control of accumulated experience. The misunderstandings of Ireland and England can be seen in some basic respects as the clash of oral and written cultures. And the strange thing to us is that the written culture has very little historical sense. The English could never remember; the Irish could never forget. Today the university as a community is in large degree one in which the members are in regular oral communication. And whereas the university has a highly developed time sense, the business community operates on the very short-run and exists mainly by the control of space. The present divorce between these two worlds is only accentuated by the perfection of the media peculiar to each.

Faced with the consequence of writing, Plato notes in the *Phaedrus:*

> This discovery of yours will create forgetfulness in the learners' souls, because they will not use their memories; they will trust to the external written characters and not remember of themselves. The specific which you have discovered is an aid not to memory, but to reminiscence and you give your disciples not truth but only the semblance of truth; they will be hearers of many things and have learned nothing; they will appear to be omniscient and will generally know nothing; they will be tiresome company, having the show of wisdom without the reality.

Two thousand years of manuscript culture lay ahead of the Western world when Plato made this observation. But nobody has yet studied the rise and decline of Greece in terms of the change from oral to written culture. Patrick Geddes said that the road destroyed the Greek city-state. But writing made the road possible, just as printing was later to pay for the roads of England and America.

In order to understand the printed-book culture which today is yielding, after four hundred years, to the impact of visual and auditory media, it is helpful to note a few of the characteristics of that manuscript culture which persisted from the 5th century B.C. to the 15th century A.D. I shall merely mention a few of the principal observations of scholars like Pierce Butler and H. J. Chaytor. In the first place, manuscript culture never made a sharp break with oral speech because everybody read manuscripts aloud. Swift, silent reading came with the macadamized surfaces of the printed page. Manuscript readers memorized most of what they read since in the nature of things they had to carry their learning with them. Fewness of manuscripts and difficulty of access made for utterly different habits of mind with regard to what was written. One result was encyclopedism. Men of learning tried, at least, to learn everything. So that if learning was oral, teaching was even more so. Solitary learning and study came only with the printed page. And today when learning and study are switching more and more to the seminar, the round-table and the discussion group, we have to note these developments as due to the decline of the printed page as the dominant art form.

The manuscript page was a very flexible affair. It was not only in close rapport with the oral speech but with plastic design and colour illustration. So the ornate examples of manuscript art easily rival and resemble those books in stone and glass, the cathedrals and abbeys. In our own time James Joyce, seeking a means to orchestrate and control the various verbi-voco-visual media of our own age, resorted to the page format of the *Book of Kells* as a means thereto. And even the early romantic poets, painters and novelists expressed their preference for gothic in terms of rebellion against book culture.

Recently Rosamund Tuve in elucidating the art of George Herbert discovered that the characteristic effects of metaphysical wit in the 17th century poetry resulted from the translation of visual effects from medieval manuscript and woodcut into the more abstract form of the printed word. If the 17th century was receding from a visual, plastic culture towards an abstract literary culture, today we seem to be receding from an abstract book culture towards a highly sensuous, plastic pictorial culture. Recent poets have used simultaneously effects from both extremes to achieve witty results not unlike those of the 17th century. The impact of Mr. Eliot's very first lines of poetry has been felt everywhere:

Let us go then, you and I,
When the evening is spread out against the sky
Like a patient etherized upon a table.

It is the overlayering of perspectives, the simultaneous use of two kinds of space which creates the shock of dislocation here. For if all art is a contrived trap for the attention, all art and all language are techniques for looking at one situation through another one.

The printed page is a 16th century art form which obliterated two thousand years of manuscript culture in a few decades. Yet it is hard for us to see the printed page or any other current medium except in contrast to some other form. The mechanical clock, for example, created a wholly artificial image of time as a uniform linear structure. This artificial form gradually changed habits of work, feeling and thought which are only being rejected today. We know that in our own lives each event exists in its own time. Time is not the same for the speaker as for the audience. To the speaker it is too, too brief for what he has to say. For the audience it is grim foretaste of eternity. Ultimately the medieval clock made Newtonian physics possible. It may also have initiated those orderly linear habits which made possible the rectilinear page of print created from movable type, as well as the methods of commerce. At any rate the mechanization of writing was as revolutionary in its consequences as the mechanization of time. And this, quite apart from thoughts or ideas conveyed by the printed page. Movable type was already the modern assembly line in embryo.

Harold Innis explored some of the consequences of the printed page: the break-down of international communication; the impetus given to nationalism by the commercial exploitation of vernaculars; the loss of contact between writers and audience; the depressing effect on music, architecture and the plastic arts.

Bela Balazs in his *Theory of the Film* notes some of the changes in visual habits resulting from the printing press on one hand and the camera on the other:

The discovery of printing gradually rendered illegible the faces of men. So much could be read from paper that the method of conveying meaning by facial expression fell into desuetude. Victor Hugo wrote once that the printed book took over the part played by the cathedral in the Middle Ages and became the carrier of the spirit of the people. But the thousands of books tore the one spirit . . . into thousands of opinions . . . tore the church into a thousand books. The visual spirit was thus turned into a legible spirit and visual culture into a culture of concepts. . . . But we paid little attention to the fact that, in conformity with this, the face of individual men, their foreheads, their eyes, their mouths, had also of necessity and quite correctly to suffer a change.

At present a new discovery, a new machine is at work to turn the attention of men back to a visual culture and to give them new faces. This machine is the cinematographic camera. Like the printing press it is a technical device for the multiplication and distribution of products of the human spirit; its effect on human culture will not be less than that of the printing press. . . . The gestures of visual man are not intended to convey concepts which can be expressed in words, but such . . . non-rational emotions which would still remain unexpressed when everything that can be told has been told. . . . Just as our musical experiences cannot be expressed in rationalized concepts, what appears on the face and in facial expression is a spiritual experience which is rendered immediately visible without the intermediary of words.

The printed page in rendering the language of the face and gesture illegible has also caused the abstract media of printed words to become the main bridge for the inter-awareness of spiritual and mental states. In the epoch of print and word culture the body ceased to have much expressive value and the human spirit became audible but invisible. The camera eye has reversed this process in reacquainting the masses of men once more within the grammar of gesture. Today commerce has channelled much of this change along sex lines. But even there the power of the camera eye to change physical attitudes and make-up is familiar to all. In the 90's Oscar Wilde noted how the pale, long-necked, consumptive red-heads painted by Rossetti and Burne-Jones were for a short time an exotic visual experience. But soon in every London salon these creatures sprouted up where none had been before. The fact that human nature, at least, imitates art is too obvious to labour. But the fact that with modern technology the entire material of the globe as well as the thoughts and feelings of its human inhabitants have become the matter of art and of man's factive intelligence means that there is no more nature. At least there is no more external nature. Everything from politics to bottle-feeding, global landscape, and the subconscious of the infant is subject to the manipulation of conscious artistic control — the BBC carries the unrehearsed voice of the nightingale to the Congo, the Eskimo sits entranced by hill-billy music from West Tennessee. Under these conditions the activities of Senator McCarthy belong with the adventures of the Pickwick Club and our talk about the Iron Curtain is a convenient smoke-screen likely to divert our attention from much greater problems. The Russians differ from us in being much more aware of the non-commercial impact of the new media. We have been so hypnotized with the commercial and entertainment qualities of press, radio, movie and TV that we have been blind to the revolutionary character of these toys. The Russians after a few years of playing with these radio-active toys have tried to neutralize them by imposing various stereotypes on their content and messages. They have forced their press to stick to an 1850 format. They have imposed similar time-locks on music and literature. They hope, thereby, to abate the revolutionary fury of these instruments. But the fury for change is in the form and not the message of the new media, a fact which seems almost inevitably to escape men trained in our abstract literary culture. The culture of print has rendered people extremely insensitive to the language and meaning of spatial forms — one reason for the architectural and city horrors tolerated by predominantly book-cultures. Thus the English and American cultures in particular were overwhelmed by print, since in the 16th century they had only rudimentary defences to set up against the new printed word. The rest of Europe, richer in plastic and oral culture, was less blitzed by the printing press. And the Orient has so far had many kinds of resistance to offer. But the curious thing is that Spaniards like Picasso or Salvador Dali are much more at home amidst the new visual culture of North America than we ourselves.

This division between visual and literary languages is a fact which has also set a great abyss between science and the humanities. Thinking as we do of culture in book terms, we are unable to read the language of technological forms. And since our earliest esthetic responses are to such forms, this has set up numerous cleavages between official and idiomatic cultural response within our own experience. We are all of us persons of divided and sub-divided sensibility through failure to recognize the multiple languages with which our world speaks to us. Above all it is the multiplicity of messages with which we are hourly bombarded by our environment that renders us ineffectual. Karl Deutsch has argued that a people shaped by oral tradition will respond to an alien challenge like a suicidal torpedo. The wild Celtic charge. A people shaped by a written tradition will not charge, but drift, pulled in a thousand different directions.

One obvious feature of the printed book is its republicanism. The page of print is not only a leveller of other forms of expression; it is a social leveller as well. Anyone who can read has at least the illusion of associating on equal terms with anyone who has written. And that fact gave the printed word a privileged place in American society and politics. The Duke of Gloucester could say casually to Edward Gibbon, on the completion of his *History*: 'Another damned fat square book. Scribble, scribble, scribble, eh, Mr. Gibbon!' But there were no fox-hunters in America to put the literary upstart in his place.

So far as quantity goes the printed book was the first instrument of mass culture. Erasmus was the first to see its meaning and turned his genius to the manufacture of textbooks for the classroom. He saw, above all, that the printing press was a device for reproducing the past in the present, much like a Hollywood movie set. The nouveaux riches of Italy began to enact on a tiny scale the past that was being unearthed and printed. Hastily they ran up villas and palazzas in ancient style. Assisted by the newly printed exemplars they began to imitate the language of Cicero and Seneca. In England the new print mingled with the old oral tradition to produce the new forms of sermon and drama which were hybrids of written and spoken culture. But in the printing press there is one great feature of mass culture which is lacking. Namely, the instantaneous. From one point of view, language itself is the greatest of all mass media. The spoken word instantly evokes not only some recently conceived idea but reverberates with the total history of its own experience with man. We may be oblivious of such overtones as of the spectrum of colour in a lump of coal. But the poet by exact rhythmic adjustment can flood our consciousness with this knowledge. The artist is older than the fish.

Reading the history of the newspaper retrospectively we can see that it was not a mere extension of the art form of the book page. As used by Rimbaud, Mallarmé and Joyce the newspaper page is a revolution in itself, juxtaposing many book pages on a single sheet. And the news page was, moreover, more nearly a mass medium not only in reaching more people than the book, but in being more instantaneous in its coverage and communication. Once linked to the telegraph, the press achieved the speed of light, as radio and TV have done since then. Total global coverage in space, instantaneity in time. Those are the two basic characters that I can detect in a mechanical mass medium. There are other characteristics derivative from these, namely anonymity of those originating the messages or forms, and anonymity in the recipients. But in respect of this anonymity it is necessary to regard not only words and metaphors as mass media but buildings and cities as well.

The modern newspaper page is not a mere extension of the book page because the speed with which the telegraph feeds news to the press today precludes any possibility of organizing a sheet of news by any but the most impressionistic devices. Each item lives in its own kind of space totally discontinuous from all other items. A particularly vigorous item will sprout a headline and provide a kind of aura or theme for surrounding items. So that, if the book page could imitate visual perspective as in Renaissance painting, setting facts and concepts in proportions that reproduced the optical image of the three-dimensional object-world, the uninhibited world of the press and modern advertising abandoned such realistic proprieties in favor of weighting news and commercial objects by every dynamic and structural device of size and colour bringing words and pictures back into a plastic and meaningful connection. If the book page tends to perspective, the news page tends to cubism and surrealism. So that every page of newspapers and magazines, like every section of our cities, is a jungle of multiple, simultaneous perspectives which make the world of hot-jazz and be-bop seem relatively sedate and classical. Our intellectual world, by virtue of the same proliferation of books (over 18,000 new titles in England alone last year) has achieved the same entanglement which is easier to assess through the complexity of our visual environment. It is not just a quantitative problem, of course. As Gyorgy Kepes states it in his *Language of Vision:*

> The environment of man living today has a complexity which cannot be compared with any environment of any previous age. The skyscrapers, the street with its kaleidoscopic vibration of colors, the window-displays with their multiple mirroring images, the street cars and motor cars, produce a dynamic simultaneity of visual impression which cannot be perceived in the terms of inherited visual habits. In this optical turmoil the fixed objects appear utterly insufficient as the measuring tape of the

events. The artificial light, the flashing of electric bulbs, and the mobile game of the many new types of light-sources bombard man with kinetic colour sensations having a keyboard never before experienced. Man, the spectator, is himself more mobile than ever before. He rides in streetcars, motorcars and aeroplanes and his own motion gives to optical impacts a tempo far beyond the threshold of a clear object-perception. The machine man operates adds its own demand for a new way of seeing. The complicated interactions of its mechanical parts cannot be conceived in a static way; they must be perceived by understanding of their movements. The motion picture, television, and, in a great degree, the radio, require a new thinking, i.e., seeing, that takes into account qualities of change, interpenetration and simultaneity.

That situation can be snapshotted from many angles. But it always adds up to the need to discover means for translating the experience of one medium or one culture into another, of translating Confucius into Western terms and Kant into Eastern terms. Of seeing our old literary culture in the new plastic terms in order to enable it to become a constitutive part of the new culture created by the orchestral voices and gestures of new media. Of seeing that modern physics and painting and poetry speak a common language and of acquiring that language at once in order that our world may possess consciously the coherence that it really has in latency, and which for lack of our recognition has created not new orchestral harmonies but mere noise.

Perhaps the terrifying thing about the new media for most of us is their inevitable evocation of irrational response. The irrational has become the major dimension of experience in our world. And yet this is a mere by-product of the instantaneous character in communication. It can be brought under rational control. It is the perfection of the means which has so far defeated the end, and removed the time necessary for assimilation and reflection. We are now compelled to develop new techniques of perception and judgement, new ways of reading the languages of our environment with its multiplicity of cultures and disciplines. And these needs are not just desperate remedies but roads to unimagined cultural enrichment.

All the types of linear approach to situations past, present or future are useless. Already in the sciences there is recognition of the need for a unified field theory which would enable scientists to use one continuous set of terms by way of relating the various scientific universes. Thus the basic requirement of any system of communication is that it be circular, with, of course, the possibility of self-correction. That is why presumably the human dialogue is and must ever be the basic form of all civilization. For the dialogue compels each participant to see and recreate his own vision through another sensibility. And the radical imperfection in mechanical media is that they are not circular. So far they have become one-way affairs with audience research taking the place of the genuine human vision, heckling and response. There is not only the anonymity of press, movies and radio but the factor of scale. The individual cannot discuss a problem with a huge, mindless bureaucracy like a movie studio or a radio corporation. On the other hand a figure like Roosevelt could mobilize the networks for a war with the press. He could even make the microphone more effective by having the press against him, because the intimacy of the microphone preserved his human dimension while the national scale of the press attack could only appear as a tank corps converging on a telephone booth.

Thus the microphone invites chat, not oratory. It is a new art form which transforms all the existing relations between speakers and their audiences and speakers and their material of discourse. 'The great rhetorical tradition which begins with Halifax and runs through Pitt to Channing, sent up its expiring flash in Macaulay.'[1] The modern manner was less declamatory and more closely reasoned. And the new manner which Gladstone handled like a Tenth Muse was based on facts and figures. Statistics represents a branch of pictorial expression. If the rise of bureaucracy and finance changed the style of public and private speech, how much more radical a change is daily worked in our habits of thought and discourse by the microphone and the loudspeaker.

Perhaps we could sum up our problem by saying that technological man must betake himself to visual metaphor in contriving a new unified language for the multiverse of cultures of the entire globe. All language or expression is metaphorical because metaphor is the seeing of one situation through another one. Right on the beam. I'll take a rain check on that.

One's vernacular is best seen and felt through another tongue. And for us, at least, society is only appreciated by comparing and contrasting it with others. Pictorial and other experience today is filled with metaphors from all the cultures of the globe. Whereas the written vernaculars have always locked men up within their own cultural monad, the language of technological man, while drawing on all the cultures of the world, will necessarily prefer those media which are least national. The language of visual form is, therefore, one which lies to hand as an unused Esperanto at everybody's command. The language of vision has already been adopted in the pictograms of scientific formula and logistics. These ideograms transcend national barriers as easily as Chaplin or Disney and would seem to have no rivals as the cultural base for cosmic man.

H. M. McLuhan

1 G. M. Young, *Victorian England*, 1944, p. 31.

THE OXFORD DICTIONARY OF NURSERY RHYMES

Edited by Iona and Peter Opie; Oxford; p. 467; $6.50

The publishers boast that this work assembles 'almost everything that is known about the subject' of nursery rhymes, and they may well be right. The book collects over five hundred rhymes, accompanying each with a bibliography of its appearances in previous collections, a few parallels in other languages, and, where possible or appropriate, a commentary. It is, apparently, the first scholarly effort at a definitive edition of them for over a century. During the century our knowledge of ballads, broadsides, folk songs, street cries and mummer plays, all of which have contributed to nursery rhymes, has made tremendous strides, so this edition is certainly overdue.

The study of nursery rhymes has been hampered by a large number of superstitions. The modern attacks on them by psychological neo-Puritans, obsessed by 'sadism' instead of sin, have had a long ancestry. We learn that in the last century a certain Goodrich climaxed thirty years of incessant campaigning against nursery rhymes by writing one for a skit, just to show how easy it was, and thus the sum of his labours was the addition of one more jingle to the canon. Then again, it is natural that infantilism of various kinds should fasten on the nursery rhyme, and the infantilism of pedantry could hardly miss. Firmly, and in some cases regretfully, the editors inform us that there is probably no connection between Jack and Jill and the gods Hjuki, and Bil of the Scandinavian Edda. (Sample of argument: 'Hjuki, in Norse, would be pronounced

Juki, which would readily become Jack; and Bil, for the sake of euphony, and in order to give a female name to one of the children, would become Jill.') That it is unlikely that the baby on the tree top is the Egyptian child-god Horus, or even the Old Pretender. That it is hardly reasonable to derive 'the cat and the fiddle' from an alleged epithet 'la Fidele' for Catherine of Aragon. That it is doubtful whether Mother Hubbard can be traced back to St. Hubert, the patron of dogs. That there is no evidence that Tommy Tucker is Cardinal Wolsey, or Simple Simon James I, or the lady riding to Banbury Cross Queen Elizabeth. The most entertaining of such speculations, the editors tell us, was a man named Ker, who a century ago undertook to prove that nursery rhymes were anti-clerical propaganda dating from the Middle Ages. His method was to translate them into a language of his own invention which he claimed to be medieval Dutch, and then re-translate them into the sentiments he wanted.

On the other hand, the editors seem willing to admit that the shoe the old woman lived in was a phallic fertility symbol (hence its use at weddings), that 'London Bridge' and 'Oranges and Lemons' may contain echoes of a distant ritual of human sacrifice, that 'Eeny, meeny, miny, mo' and 'Hickory, Dickory, Dock' are numerals of long-extinct Celtic languages, and that a few rhymes may have once had political allusions. Sometimes the editors are over-cautious and inconclusive, as well as too coy about the 'indelicate' variants of their canon. But by presenting the bibliographical evidence clearly and in order, they do give us, in nearly every case, a kind of minimum working basis for any future theories. They dispose of the claim that the 'Mairzy Doats' song of a few years ago was a spontaneous production of somebody's little girl by placidly tracing it back to the year 1450. They demolish the legend about the origin of 'Mary Had a Little Lamb' which caused Henry Ford to restore what he thought was the school where those two maudlin infants had turned up, and to have a book published on the subject. They have tracked down and identified several of those stray wisps of song and jingle which everyone knows, and nobody knows the origin of. (I seem to remember that it was a major effort of detection to locate the author of 'Sweet Adeline', not of course in the present collection, who turned out to be a serious-minded composer greatly chagrined to find that his song had become the great national anthem of drunks.) From this dictionary we learn that 'Where, O Where is My Little Dog Gone?' is the first stanza of a comic German-dialect ballad of the nineteenth century which ends as follows:

Un sausage ish goot, boloney of course,
Oh where, oh where can he be?
Dey makes un mit dog and dey makes em mit horse,
I guess dey makes em mit he.

We learn that the pig stolen by Tom the piper's son was a candy pig, that Miss Muffet's tuffet is more likely to be a grassy knoll than a three-legged stool, which is also possible, and that the old man thrown down the stairs was a daddy-long-legs.

The editors make it clear that, while some nursery rhymes were originally written for children, many come from the first stanza or two of popular songs that have been remembered by some hard-pressed mother or nurse, and, once brought into contact with children, preserved by the extraordinary conservatism of children that keeps calling for the same thing over and over without permitting a syllable's change. Sometimes a popular song or ballad will develop from a nursery rhyme, and the popularity of the song confirms the status of the nursery rhyme: this happened with 'If I had a donkey that wouldn't go' and may have happened with 'Old Mother Hubbard'. The whole subject of nursery rhymes is far broader than that very British and middle-class institution of the nursery, and its problems are the problems of all popular and oral literature.

The subject has another importance too. Nursery rhymes are not only the best possible introduction to poetry; they represent almost the only genuine poetic experience that many people ever get. The child of three who is bounced on somebody's knee to the rhythm of 'Ride a Cock Horse' is beginning to learn what poetry is. It is interesting to notice how much he does not need. He does not need a footnote telling him that Banbury Cross is twenty miles north of Oxford. He does not need the information that 'cross' and 'horse' make not a rhyme but an assonance. He certainly needs no guesswork identifying the fine lady with Queen Elizabeth or Lady Godiva or (by virtue of a pun that started as a leg-pull) Celia Fiennes. But, for one brief moment, he has participated in the intense physical ecstasy that poetry shares with music and the dance, the ecstasy of the thundering hexameters of Homer, the galloping alliteration of Beowulf, the sinewy blank verse that was bellowed at the noisy and restless audience of the Globe Theatre. Then he goes to school and discovers that poetry is really an unnatural and perverse way of distorting ordinary prose statements, and so of course loses interest. It is unlikely that his interest will be reawakened, either, unless he comes across something that can appeal to the childhood memory which lies buried deep in his stomach muscles. If he has been so completely processed by dull educational theory or sharp commercial practice that he has missed out even on nursery rhymes, there should be nothing to disturb his adjustment to reality, however dingy and foolish a reality it may be.

Northrop Frye

NOTES ON THE CONTRIBUTORS

DAVID BIDNEY, Associate Professor of Anthropology and Philosophy, Indiana University, is the author of *Theoretical Anthropology* published by Columbia and Oxford University Presses this Fall.

EDMUND LEACH, Professor of Anthropology, Cambridge University, has done fieldwork in China, Formosa, Iraq, Burma, and Borneo. The Curl Prize was awarded to him in 1951 for his essay 'The Structural Implications of Matrilateral Cross-cousin Marriage.' *Journal of the Royal Anthropological Institute,* 81:23-55. He will soon publish a book on time concepts in various societies.

JOHN CARRINGTON lives in an isolated station at Yalemba, Basoko, Province Orientale, Belgian Congo, where he is in charge of a boys' school of the Baptist Missionary Society. He received his Ph.D. in anthropology from the University of London.

DAVID RIESMAN, Professor of Social Sciences, University of Chicago, and author of *The Lonely Crowd* and *Faces in the Crowd,* now heads the Kansas City Study of Middle-Age and Aging. He was law clerk to the late Justice Brandeis and Visiting Professor of Law at Yale. This Spring he will be at Johns Hopkins.

ROBERT GRAVES recently published *The Nazarene Gospel Restored* in collaboration with Joshua Podro and *Greek Myth and Pseudo-Myth.* Since 1929 he has made his home on the outskirts of a Majorcan mountain-village.

HANS SELYE, Professor of Physiology, Université de Montréal, gained international fame with his book *Stress.*

GYORGY KEPES, Professor of Visual Design at the Massachusetts Institute of Technology, is the author of *Language of Vision* and the forthcoming book *The New Landscape.*

MELFORD SPIRO, Associate Professor of Anthropology, University of Connecticut, has done fieldwork in Micronesia and Israel.

ANTHONY HORNECK's translation of the Mohra trial was Cotton Mather's 'favorite Swedish case.'

RALPH GOODMAN is the pseudonym of an executive in the American advertising industry. His article is reprinted from *The Nation,* 176:7.

H. M. MCLUHAN, Professor of English, St. Michael's College, University of Toronto, is the author of *The Mechanical Bride.*

G. LEGMAN of New York is the author of *Love and Death* and other books.

NORTHROP FRYE, Chairman of the Department of English, Victoria College, University of Toronto, and author of *Fearful Symmetry: A Study of William Blake,* is now writing a book on the *Faerie Queene.* In the Spring he will be Visiting Professor of English at Princeton. His review is reprinted from the *Canadian Forum.*

The cover illustration comes from *The Loon's Necklace,* a film produced by Crawley Films and released by Imperial Oil Limited.

www.ingramcontent.com/pod-product-compliance
Lightning Source LLC
Chambersburg PA
CBHW070921270326
41927CB00011B/2672
9781620324271